AS MANY AS THE STARS

AS MANY AS THE STARS

A Story of Change
for the Children of China

Robert Glover OBE

With Theodore Brun

HODDER &
STOUGHTON

First published in Great Britain in 2020 by Hodder & Stoughton
An Hachette UK company

1

A CIP catalogue record for this title
is available from the British Library

Hardback ISBN 978 1 529 31717 6
eBook ISBN 978 1 529 31719 0

Typeset in Celeste by Palimpsest Book Production Ltd, Falkirk, Stirlingshire

Printed and bound in Great Britain by Clays Ltd, Elcograf S.p.A.

Hodder & Stoughton policy is to use papers that are natural, renewable
and recyclable products and made from wood grown in sustainable forests.
The logging and manufacturing processes are expected to conform
to the environmental regulations of the country of origin.

Hodder & Stoughton Ltd
Carmelite House
50 Victoria Embankment
London EC4Y 0DZ

www.hodderfaith.com

Thank you to my brave and courageous wife Elizabeth and my children Rachel, Lois, Megan, Anna, Joel and Joshua, who were equally called by God for the journey to China. We could only have gone to China together, all sharing the risk, challenges and sacrifices. Together we received rich blessings from our Father who continues to lead us on an exciting, exhilarating life of faith and prayer.

Lots of love Dad

Contents

Preface

---

*'Look up at the sky and count the stars – if indeed you can
count them.' Then he said to him, 'So shall your offspring be.'*
(Genesis 15:5)

This is a story about many things, about many people. But above all, it is about the father heart of God. It is a story that shows that God has a plan for each of us and an adventure into which he calls those who are willing to risk – well, everything.

If you go outside one night under a clear sky and gaze up at the stars, could you begin to count them, as the Lord charged Abraham to do? Would you even try? This is a story about stars, too, and fathers, and those without them.

I was one of those.

My father left his family when I was two. I never knew him. I don't remember anything about him from that time. Maybe God has a sense of irony – in fact, I'm sure he does – that he should take a man who had no father and make him a father to so many. Or maybe it takes a man who had no father to know the value of surrounding every child with a loving family.

It's been my privilege to play a part in a story that God wanted to tell, in a plan he intended to execute, in China. This is the story I want to tell you. Why he called me, a lad from Norfolk, to help bring about a revolution in childcare on the other side of the world, I can't say. But he did. And to a nation with a one-child policy he chose to send Liz and me, who had six children: that brought many laughs with officials in China. And now that multitude of orphans, whom he has placed in the care of loving fathers and mothers all over that teeming nation, number as many as the stars . . .

1: First Contact

In their hearts humans plan their course,
but the Lord establishes their steps.
(Proverbs 16:9)

Even now, in the twenty-first century, you would be hard pressed to think of two places more different than Shanghai and Norfolk. One with its thronging multitudes and dusty exhaust-clogged air, every day sprouting another towering spike of steel and glass; the other with its sleepy market towns and flint-stone villages, its big, clean skies and pale, windswept beaches. But in the 1960s, there really was no comparison. They were different worlds.

I was thirteen years old when, for me, these two worlds first touched. At the time, my mother, my two sisters and I were living in a small semi-detached house on Denton Road in Norwich. I was attending a school called Alderman Jex – a place I had dreaded as a younger boy walking home from my junior school down the road because the older kids from Alderman's would chase us and beat us up if they caught us. I had passed my 11+ examination, which in those days meant I had an open ticket to one of the grammar schools on the south side of Norwich. But, even having cleared that hurdle, my family couldn't afford the daily bus fare across town, so it was Alderman Jex and its bullies for me. Swallowing my fears, I settled into life there as best I could.

Then, one day, a new boy turned up in class. He was Chinese. The teacher said he came from Hong Kong and that his name was Yuk Leung Yau. One of the children at the back of the class made retching noises, thinking he was being funny, and was told to pipe down. Then our new classmate was invited to say something about his home city. It was soon pretty clear that he didn't know much English.

I felt sorry for him, though some of the other lads sniggered at his halting efforts and his accent and pulled faces behind his back. In the late 1960s, anything but a white Caucasian was a rare sight in Norwich. I remember a set of triplets who were the mixed-heritage children of a local Norfolk girl who had fallen for an African–American GI stationed there in the 1950s. But faces from the Far East were unknown.

Children being children, the teasing continued after class and I could see on the Chinese boy's face how the jibes were hitting their mark. I guessed he must have been feeling pretty lonely as it was, and the other boys were only making it worse.

'How would you like it if you were the only white kid in a Chinese class?' I said, squaring up to the ringleader. I was still pretty skinny myself at that age, so I think it was probably surprise that I had stood up to him more than a sudden pang of conscience that made the bully back off, and I was left standing alone in the corridor with the Chinese kid.

'Thank you,' he said, ducking his head of jet-black hair.

'What d'you say your name was?' My own Norfolk accent was pretty broad in those days.

'Yuk Leung Yau,' he replied.

I frowned. 'Hmm. How about I just call you Jimmy?' And so Jimmy he was to us, ever after.

Jimmy and I became good friends. It turned out his family had moved to Norwich to start the first Chinese restaurant in the city. Even at that time, Britain was still recovering from the effects of the Second World War, and rationing had only ended a few years before, so the idea of Chinese cuisine in Norfolk seemed impossibly exotic.

I would visit Jimmy often. His house was full of pots of bean sprouts that his dad used as ingredients in his restaurant. He would give us banana fritters as snacks, for which I soon developed quite a passion. After all, bananas had only been available in England for a few years, but no one ate them fried like that.

'I think I'd like to visit China when I'm older,' I announced to Jimmy one morning in an art class. 'You reckon you can teach me some Chinese?'

Jimmy was busy on his drawing. 'Some other time,' he said, concentrating on a particularly delicate detail. He was by far the best artist in class.

'Go on,' I persisted, jogging his arm. 'Teach me something.'

He threw down his pencil and scowled. 'Okay, okay. Say *moho te sing*.'

'Mo-ho . . . tay . . . sing,' I repeated in my flat Norfolk tones. 'What's it mean?'

'"Shut up" in Cantonese,' he replied. I guess that told me. Even so, I walked around school the next few days muttering '*moho te sing*' to myself, trying to get it right, much to Jimmy's amusement.

I can't say why exactly, but something about China and the Chinese people fascinated me from early on, although they had nothing to do with my life in Norfolk. And for a long while I cherished a secret promise to myself that, one day, I'd visit there. One day . . .

But all that lay some distance in the future. Meanwhile, the focus of my teenage years was not China, not faith, but – like a lot of young boys, I guess – football.

When I was a small boy, my mother's long-standing friend Ted, who eventually became her husband, often took me to Carrow Road. This was the home of Norwich City Football Club, better known as The Canaries, and I used to adore watching them play (I still do). At the time, they were one of the top teams in the country, playing in the nation's First Division. The players were like gods to me – men like Kevin Keelan, the 'greatest goalkeeper not to get an international cap' (as he was born in India), and the brawny Scottish defender Duncan Forbes. So when I was a bit older and four of us lads from Alderman Jex first eleven were invited to try out for the Norwich City squad, I thought my moment of destiny had arrived.

For a few sweet months, I trained at Norwich City training

ground at Trowse. I was still skinny, but what I lacked in bulk I made up for in enthusiasm. Despite our young age, we trained with the senior players two evenings a week. I remember, at a few sessions, Kevin Keelan would take a ten-bob note off each new youth player and invite us to shoot penalties at him for practice. If he saved more than five penalties out of ten, he got to keep all the money. If not, he would give us back our note and pay each of us ten bob out of his own pocket, whether or not we had scored. Needless to say, we never won a farthing. Still, I loved it. This was my future, I was sure of it. But then the new season came around and the coach told me I was still too slight to be of any use to them. 'Come back next year,' he said, trying to sound encouraging, 'after you've done some growing.'

I was heartbroken. Tears streamed down my face as I cycled home from the ground that day, my dream of playing for The Canaries crushed beyond repair.

There was another brief glimpse of hope when the coach of Colchester United, Ray Crawford, invited me to train with them. But Colchester were only a Third-Division side and it took me an hour on the train to journey south to play with them each session. My heart wasn't in it. It was The Canaries or nothing for me, and when Ted pointed out that I wasn't going to make a living playing for second-rate teams like Colchester United anyway, I knew he was right. I needed a real job.

The best Plan B I could come up with was to join the Royal Navy. I craved adventure. It was time to see the world, and the recruitment posters promised that I surely would. But first, it seemed, I had to have another dream shattered.

I had decided that, since I stood on the threshold of manhood, the time had come to meet my father. I was sixteen and I had questions that I wanted answered. The older I got, the more questions I had. Why had he left us? Why had he and Mum divorced? And, more fundamentally, what sort of a man was he? Yet, although I was curious for answers, I think some deeper part of me recognised that even having them wouldn't make a real difference and couldn't fill the hole he had left behind.

At the time, he was living in the market town of Ormskirk, near Liverpool. He had another family by then – two more sons, both quite young. He came to pick me up from the station. I watched an average-looking man in a raincoat with greying hair get out of a car and approach me. It was a strange, hollow feeling. Underwhelming. I wasn't angry. In fact, I didn't feel any emotional connection to him at all, although I had thought I would.

The visit was pleasant enough. He tried to make me feel as comfortable and welcomed as possible. His new wife, Rhona, did the same. His two boys – my half-brothers, aged six and four – rode in the car with us. They were wide-eyed when I pulled out a carton of cigarettes and lit up on the drive to their home, thinking I was impossibly grown up. But I was just a kid like them.

For all my father's kindness, it turned out that the years apart from each other couldn't be bridged. He wasn't the hero of my boyish daydreams. He wasn't the missing piece in my heart, after all. I'd have to look for that elsewhere – if it existed at all.

That doesn't mean this realisation wasn't painful. Every boy needs a father, and anyone who tells you otherwise doesn't understand the truth. There had been many occasions on the football field when I had longed to hear a father's voice cheering me on, even though Mum did her best. And I couldn't fail to notice how often the other children's fathers had a word in the coach's ear on their behalf. I'd had no one like that to speak up for me and, at that stage, I certainly didn't know how to speak up for myself, because no father had ever taught me how, or given me the confidence I needed to do so.

Later, I found out more about him, which he didn't tell me then. He had served behind enemy lines during the Second World War. He was gifted with languages and had spent years involved in secret operations in Belgium, Holland and France. He had seen some pretty shocking things, which he described in his memoirs.

Discovering this helped me to understand the man and the choices he had later made, to understand that the notion of living a double life had been ingrained in him, so much so that when he came back to peacetime, why wouldn't he carry on his intrigues? One life wasn't enough for him.

For all that, perhaps my father did pass one trait on to me, after all: a longing for adventure. And that was what I was hoping for when I signed up for the Royal Navy.

As a brand-new naval 'rating' – the lowest rank in the Navy – I was sent for basic training to HMS *Ganges* on the Suffolk coast in the village of Shotley, a so-called boys' training establishment. When it came to the physical exercises, assault courses and so on, the intensity was a shock at first, but I soon got used to them and rose to the challenges, until finally I came to love them. As well as all the usual stuff, I was allowed to play football, first for a ratings side and soon, having been selected up the various levels, I found myself playing for the Navy against the other armed services. With this came a certain degree of respect. I stood out from the other ratings and became a known face among the senior officers. I'd be lying if I said I didn't enjoy that.

Things changed a bit after basic training, though. I was sent to HMS *Pembroke*, a naval base in Chatham, Kent, where I trained in the supply and secretarial trade. Not quite the adventure I had signed up for. Still, I hoped that when it came to my posting I would get something more exciting. My goal, of course, was still the Far East. My interest in China had not waned, and I thought that if the Navy would pay me to get out there, so much the better.

So, after my passing out, I put in a draft request for an aircraft carrier or a destroyer. A letter soon arrived from the drafting officer, saying, 'Welcome to the Submarine Command as a volunteer.' I quickly wrote back saying that there must be some mistake, that I certainly hadn't volunteered for Submarine Command, and repeated my request to be posted to a destroyer. A terse reply followed, welcoming me to Submarine Command, this time as a 'non-volunteer'. It looked like I was going to be a submariner whether I liked it or not.

And so, instead of cruising the balmy waters of the South China Sea, I resigned myself to the fact that I would be lurking in the freezing depths of the Baltic and North Seas, crammed inside a metal tube. Like Jonah in the belly of the whale.

> *Out of the depths I cry to you,* LORD.
> (Psalm 130:1)

When I passed out into the Royal Navy, the world was still firmly in the grip of the Cold War. During the course of my service, I served on two different Oberon-class submarines – HMS *Oberon* herself and HMS *Opossum*. They were deployed to do essentially two opposite tasks. The first was to patrol British waters and locate, pursue and see off any Soviet submarines caught infiltrating friendly waters. The second was on reconnaissance in the Baltic, photographing Soviet naval movements in and out of the various naval bases they had positioned around the eastern rim of that sea, which often meant working in concert with the SBS, or Special Boat Service (the British equivalent of the US Navy Seals). In the latter case, we were the ones being chased away, usually with depth charges. And cold though the war may have officially been, the charges were real enough, and potentially deadly to any boat compromised six hundred feet below the surface.

On each tour, we would spend several months at sea. The conditions were not designed for a man like me. By then I had grown into a strapping lad of six foot two. The highest point in the middle of an Oberon-class submarine was six feet. So you can imagine how I soon had a fine collection of cuts and bruises on the top of my head when I forgot to stoop low enough to pass through a hatch.

Besides the confined space, there were seventy men living in our diesel-electric submarine, so conditions were not easy. Each rating had a locker assigned to him in which to keep his few possessions, but only the senior ratings were allocated a bunk. Junior ratings had to 'hot bunk'. This meant when your duty shift was over and it was your turn to sleep, you simply grabbed whatever bunk was available. We couldn't wash either, because after two weeks at sea, all water supplies were preserved for drinking. When the sub was on the surface, it ran on diesel and the whole place would fill with the fumes, so before long every man was coated with diesel grime and living on stale air that stank of body odour and cigarette smoke. It was grim.

The crew was pretty grim, too. The language was coarse, the jokes blue and the bullying relentless, especially for a junior rating like me, and on shore the drinking was harder than any I've known before or since.

Despite all this, eventually I *settled* in, even if I didn't exactly *fit* in. Living in close quarters with so many people beneath the ocean waves is intense. You learn what you need to do to survive. And I think this was where I learned a different approach to difficult people. I started to understand how they operate, to see what it is that makes different people react differently to the same situation. For example, not everyone could handle being cooped up with that many other men, unable to escape them, and a few of the new submariners faked claustrophobia to get out. I can't say I enjoyed it much myself, but I stuck out my time.

The hazards were real. Above all, there was always the risk of a breach in the hull, and we drilled relentlessly for such an eventuality. Speed was of the essence. If seawater were ever to penetrate the hull at depth, the crew would have only seconds to isolate the breach by closing the hatches either side of the compromised compartment if the vessel were to survive. Once secure, the procedure was to 'blow' the main ballast tank, the Q Tank. That meant forcing high-pressure air into the forward tanks, forcing out the ballast water and thereby instantly lightening the fore ends of the boat so that it would rise to the surface like the kraken, at a near vertical angle. At this point, we needed to be holding on to something tight, because everything not tied down would come raining down through the upended compartments. Any man who didn't make it out of the isolated compartment would become a regrettable but necessary sacrifice in order to safeguard the lives of the rest of the crew. Needless to say, this sharpened our reaction speed to a fine point whenever an alarm – for drill or for real – was sounded.

Many times in the Baltic on HMS *Oberon*, we lay on the seabed in total silence while overhead Soviet gunboats and minesweepers on patrol searched for our position. They were times to fray a man's nerves, I can tell you. The Russians would drop speculative depth charges to try to flush us out. We could hear them explode above us, or off at some distance, and feel the reverberations shake through the structure of the sub, and we would pray that the Russians wouldn't score a more direct hit by sheer luck and cause us serious damage.

But the most serious incident during my service wasn't hiding from depth charges. It came at the end of my first week at sea. I was sound asleep when I was startled awake to find water gushing into my bunk. The tannoy blared out, 'Safeguard, safeguard, safeguard, flooding in the after ends!' The word 'safeguard' meant it wasn't a drill. I scrambled out of the bunk, knowing that, because we were at depth and if the breach were serious, this could be it for all of us. Because I had been off duty and asleep, most of the other crew members were out of the after ends before me and the door was about to be sealed. If I was too late, I would be trapped: collateral damage, better left to drown than risk the lives of the entire crew.

The atmosphere was fraught and I was moving as fast as I could, but I remember feeling an unearthly peace come over me like a shield. 'Help me, Jesus! Help me!' I murmured under my breath. Even as I said it, I had a sort of vision of him standing there beside me, and somehow I knew I would be all right. The water was rushing past at knee height, but I managed to squeeze

out through the hatch before they closed it. I was the last man
out.

It was only later that we discovered it hadn't been seawater
filling the submarine; rather, the fresh water tank had burst. A
much less serious emergency, although we still needed to surface
at once, and fortunately all turned out well.

I suppose this is a fair indication of where my faith stood at
this stage in my life. In mortal danger? Yep. Time to cry out to
God. Anything short of that and my faith tended to take a bit of
a back seat, especially among the crew. On leave back home in
Norwich, I would still attend church with my mother and I would
have called myself a Christian if anyone had asked. But no one
did. And it never would have occurred to me to share my faith
with anyone else, least of all the tough bunch of submariners I
worked with.

However, there was another crew member who took a different
approach. His name was Brown. He wore his faith on his sleeve
and talked about Jesus to anyone who would listen, and to quite
a few who didn't want to. As a result, he drew a lot of flak from
the other crew members and he was bullied pretty badly. One
trick I remember them playing on him was 'blowing the slop'
while he was in the 'head' (toilet). Normal procedure is to shut
down the valves on all the toilets before doing this or you'd be
standing in a shower of sewage. But that was the point. Poor
Brown. He was covered head to toe in human waste. And all for
Jesus.

I told him to tone down his evangelising so that the crew bullies
would leave him alone, but he wouldn't listen. Even though I
thought it foolish at the time, I could see his faith meant more
to him than his reputation, and a part of me admired that. It
would be a long time before my faith began to look anything like
his.

I decided to leave the Navy when I was twenty-one, still harbouring
dreams of somehow making it as a professional footballer. For a

short while during and after working out my notice, I secured a position playing professionally for Portsmouth Football Club, thanks to connections with the coach, Ray Crawford, who knew me from my brief stint at Colchester. But the glimpse of a new career and new aspirations was short-lived. Playing at home at Fratton Park, I did a slide tackle and my left knee collided with the goalpost. The blow smashed my knee and left me in a full leg cast for the next three months. When it came off, the muscles were wasted and I was told it would be another full year before I could even play football again.

That was it, the end of my footballing career, once and for all. In hindsight, I can't say I deeply lament it, but at the time I felt crushed, and I returned home to Norfolk to regroup. But here again was a repeat of a recurring pattern in my life. I had grand designs to forge ahead on a certain path, only to find those plans thwarted and my course turned in another direction, heading towards where God wanted me to be. In this particular case, I'm very glad he did.

2: Getting My Attention

A wife of noble character who can find?
She is worth far more than rubies.
(Proverbs 31:10)

I found a job pretty quickly upon my return to Norwich, working as an accountant for a company called Anglia Windows. It sounds dry enough, but in fact the business was something of rags-to-riches story for the man who had started it, and there was certainly a buzz about the place. However, it was soon clear to me that sitting in an office under hideously stark strip lights was not for me, so I didn't linger long.

Instead, I applied for a job in a school for difficult teenagers in the nearby town of Sheringham, perched on the North Norfolk coast. The place was called the Sheringham Court School for Maladjusted Boys. Quite a mouthful, and quite a change for me – although it wasn't such a left-field decision as it first might seem following the Navy.

The role essentially meant I would be the boys' physical education teacher, which made sense, given my footballing background. But it also involved duties as a 'house father' – in other words, overseeing the boys' after-school activities a couple of times a week and ensuring that, on those evenings, they all ate, washed and got to bed in good order.

Not long after I started my new job at the school I met a fisherman called Andrew at the Crown Inn, one of the pubs in Sheringham. We struck up a bit of a friendship. He took me out on his boat once or twice over the summer to catch crabs and lobsters. Afterwards he would invite me for supper with his family, who lived in the little village of Weybourne, down the road from

Sheringham. It was there that I met his younger sister, Elizabeth. With blonde hair, blue eyes and high, sharp cheekbones, she looked to me like a Norse goddess (and still does). She was only seventeen at the time, so I didn't pay her much attention at first, being twenty-four myself. But it wasn't long before my interest grew, and soon I realised that Elizabeth April Roper was going to be the love of my life.

It says in the book of Proverbs, 'Houses and wealth are inherited from parents, but a prudent wife is from the LORD' (Proverbs 19:14). I didn't have an earthly father in my life, but if God chose Liz for me, he certainly knew what he was doing. Meeting her was the most important event of my life, as you will see.

As our courtship unfolded, I was learning more and more about my new career in social care. Not all of it was good: some of it was downright shocking. Sheringham Court School had boys sent to it from all over the country. So-called 'troublemakers' or 'difficult children', exiled to Norfolk to keep them out of the way – at least, that was the theory. Most of them had been referred to the school through the courts. But if they might have caused a bit of trouble before, some were certainly more likely to do so after a short stint at the school.

Youngsters would be sent to Sheringham for all kinds of reasons, but usually it was because the problem was with the child, not with their social environment, as would be the case in other residential care homes I later worked in. Usually the boys had been in trouble with the law: shoplifting, stealing a car or joyriding, or getting mixed up with drugs. But if they arrived with one problem, they soon learned from the other boys a dozen other ways to get into trouble. Rather like first offenders entering prison for a few months for some fairly minor offence and then being schooled in far more serious criminal activity, so it was often the case with these boys. You could see them becoming institutionalised almost from the first day. The official statistics were depressing: of persistent offenders between the ages of seventeen and twenty-one, around 80 per cent had been in care.

From the beginning I tried to adopt a fresh approach. One of the first activities I organised was a series of boxing bouts. It probably wouldn't have passed health and safety these days. I wore one glove and gave the other to each boy in turn and we sparred for a minute or two until it was clear who was the winner – invariably me. One by one I went through them, going fairly easy on them, until at last there were only the three main kingpins from among the older boys left. These were pretty hefty lads of seventeen or eighteen, hardened by petty crime or tough living in Birmingham and London, with bulging biceps and a gleam in their eye that said they would be the one to show the teacher who was really the boss.

Those three bouts nearly killed me! But I was determined to win their admiration and establish my authority, and one by one I gained the upper hand. By the end of the session, even Lenny from the East End – the toughest one of all – was willing to grant me grudging respect.

On another of my first nights as a house father, I had to organise an activity for the evening. I was told that the boys were usually given things like balsa-wood model-making to do, or crafting tie-dye T-shirts. Even to me, that sounded dull as ditchwater – no wonder they were all so restless. So instead, I threw them in the school minivan and told them we were off to catch rats. I armed them all with small clubs and, of course, talked up the size of the rats on the drive over.

'How big?' the boys asked, wide-eyed.

'Oh, big as a Norfolk terrier, at least,' I lied. I gave them each a piece of binder twine to tie around the bottom of their trousers to stop these 'monster' rats running up their legs.

An hour or so of them chasing around in the dark tired them out all right, and when I got them back to their sleeping quarters, they had their cocoa and got to bed in double-quick time and were all settled and quiet by lights out. The headmaster couldn't understand what had happened.

'How on earth did you do it?' he asked, stunned to find the place so quiet when he did the rounds that night.

The simple answer was that I just asked myself what I would like to do if I were in their place. It certainly wouldn't be making tie-dye T-shirts. I've often found that to be a helpful approach – to put myself in the other person's shoes and try to see things from their side. It helped me make sense of some otherwise quite inexplicable decisions on their parts.

By now, I knew I wanted to live near the Ropers – well, near Liz anyway. So I applied for a job as a residential social worker at a children's home a few miles along the coast from Weybourne. The Grange children's home had about thirty children.

These children were a little different from those at Sheringham Court. They were usually there because of social problems in their family environment, rather than because they themselves had done something wrong. Often, they were the children of parents with alcoholism or drug addiction; sometimes there had been complaints and investigations of sexual abuse, general neglect, and so on – things that, in general, were not their own fault. But it didn't alter the fact that, once in residential care, whether good or bad themselves, they soon started to pick up bad traits from the others.

What shocked me the most, however, was how easily children with two perfectly good parents could end up in the social care system. It felt in those days as though social workers had a hair trigger when it came to referring teenagers into institutionalised care, whereas it seemed blindingly obvious to me that it was far better for a child to be raised within the context of a family situation, even one that was far from perfect, rather than to be stuck in an institution where not only would their behaviour suffer, being exposed to and influenced by other children with a welter of other problems, but their mentality would also change. They would come to feel safer *inside* an institution than out of one. And, to me, that was not a good state to be in.

Worse than that, I found that some of the parents seemed to take a perverse pride in their son (in most cases, it was a boy) being sent away to a home like The Grange, as if it were a kind of rite of passage that every boy ought to go through. I remember one father railing at me when I suggested that I could see no good reason why his son should come into our care but that he should stay at home. 'His grandfather lived in a home,' he fumed. 'I lived in a home, and he's going to damn well do his time in a home as well.'

Many times I sat through someone listing a litany of 'problems' about a particular kid, and I'd have to bite my tongue to stop myself from blurting, 'Can't you see? He's just a normal teenager!'

I couldn't help feeling, in many cases, that parents had shirked their responsibilities to raise their adolescent children, and that the system made it far too easy for them to do this. I couldn't get my head around the idea that parents could turn up at weekends, take their children out for an ice cream and a stroll along the seafront, and then drop them off in the home again. For children to be treated as an inconvenience was, to my mind, nothing short of scandalous.

Meanwhile, more happily, Liz and I got engaged in December 1983. We were married in April the following year in the little parish church in Weybourne, a week after Liz's twentieth birthday. We bought a two-bedroom bungalow in Sheringham with a decent garden. Liz was training to be a nurse and I had obtained a two-day-a-week concession from The Grange to study at Norwich City College for my Certificate in Social Services.

Our first child, Rachel, was born on 5 May 1985. I was as besotted with my little blonde-haired girl as I was with my wife. Life was good. I loved my family. I felt fulfilled in my career. It gave me great confidence to know that I was carrying myself and my young family forward in life, relying on little but my own energy and strength of will.

But things were about to change.

Suddenly a sound like the blowing of a violent wind came from heaven and filled the whole house where they were sitting.

(Acts 2:2)

I'd be surprised if you've heard of a condition called Guillain-Barré syndrome, a disorder of the nervous system. I certainly hadn't when it struck me down. But, thank God, Liz had.

When Rachel was about six months old, I was walking up the steps to City College when suddenly my legs gave way. Although I could still move them, I had a horrible sensation of pins and needles in my legs and hands and realised quickly it was something serious.

By the time I'd got myself home to bed, I had developed flu-like symptoms as well as numbness. The doctor told Liz to give me a paracetamol and put me to bed for a few days. However, luckily for me, as part of her nursing training Liz happened to have done a study on an old lady who had died from Guillain-Barré syndrome. Paralysis begins in the feet and hands, and then spreads to the lungs and the heart. If it reaches that stage, it is likely to be fatal.

Liz was convinced that this was what I had, although at first she didn't tell me of her suspicions. If I had it, she knew there was an 80 per cent chance that I would end up with a disability – or worse, that I could die. When I couldn't get out of bed, she called an ambulance.

Within a short space of time, I found myself languishing on a ward in the Norfolk and Norwich Hospital 'under observation'. It was the most depressing place I'd ever been in, and made the cramped innards of an SO9 submarine seem positively airy by comparison. The air was stifling and the atmosphere morbid, and with good reason. The ward was full of old men suffering from various conditions, but in general they were mostly on the way out. Every morning another bed was empty, and when I asked the nurse where its occupant had gone, I was told he had died in the night.

Meanwhile, my 'observation' entailed a consultant coming round and sticking a pin in my leg, starting at my toes and gradually working his way upwards until I let out a yelp, finally feeling something beyond the rising tide of paralysis. The odd thing about this was that it was literally the fulfilment of a recurring nightmare I had had as a child: I used to dream about a man in a white coat peering in at my window, brandishing a long and fiendishly sharp needle, which he obviously wanted to stick in me. The reality wasn't much less disturbing.

Of course, all the while, Liz was under tremendous pressure, managing with Rachel on her own and worried about me. Neither of us had any active faith at the time, so we just sort of gutted it out for a while in our own strength.

But then things took a turn for the worse. The doctors gave me a lumbar puncture so that my consultant could investigate more, but I had a very negative reaction to it, which meant my back was in constant pain, and each time I sat up I felt as if my head was exploding. I started acting out of character and didn't make any sense – which put the wind up Liz and my mother when they visited me. The thing that drove my mother over the edge, I'm told, was when I used the urine bottle in front of her. 'Something is seriously wrong,' she whispered to Liz. 'Robert would *never* do that!'

As they left the hospital, Liz turned to Mum with tears in her eyes. 'Am I losing him?' she murmured.

Ever practical, Mum realised they had to do something. The following day I was due to have an X-ray on my back, so Mum decided they should call a prayer meeting at her church to pray for me. Liz, although she might have called herself a Christian at the time, had no real faith of her own or experience of God, but she was happy to go along with Mum's plan, if only because it meant she was doing something active to help me.

The next day an attendant came to wheel me down to the X-ray unit. I was relieved simply to be getting out of the ward, even for a short time, despite the pain I was in. They left me parked in the corridor awaiting my eleven o'clock appointment, feeling tired, irritable and in constant pain.

How had life led me to this? Everything had been going according to plan – well, according to my plan, at least – but now I seemed to have hit a brick wall. I couldn't even get out of bed. It was humiliating. Forget about my limbs; my spirit was broken. All I could do was lie there and feel sorry for myself.

From where I lay, waiting, I could see a big, black clock above the double doors that flapped open and shut whenever someone was coming or going from the unit. Suddenly, when the clock read exactly 11.00 a.m., the doors opened wide – but no one came through them. Only a sudden blast of sweet, fresh air washed past me. I gulped down a big lungful of the stuff.

Ahhh – beautiful, I sighed to myself, and instantly I felt better. It was a few seconds more before I realised the headache I had been enduring for weeks had vanished.

When Liz and my mother visited me later that day, they couldn't believe how different I appeared.

'You look great,' exclaimed Liz. 'How are you feeling?'

'Pretty good, I have to say,' I replied. And then I told them what had happened. Liz and Mum exchanged glances.

'What time was this?' asked Liz, hesitantly.

So I told her: eleven o'clock exactly. I knew from the clock on the wall.

Their mouths fell open. 'But that's extraordinary,' said Liz. 'That's the exact time we were praying for your healing.'

Amazing as it was, I suddenly felt ashamed. I had cried out to God in that submarine, but in this illness I had just sat there, inert as a brick, suffering, and without it ever occurring to me to ask God for help. Instead it had taken my wife and mother to do that.

Eventually we figured out that it wasn't just life-or-death situations that we had to pray for. Later, in China, we learned pretty quickly to cover everything in prayer. But, for now, there I was, witness to something extraordinary, something apparently supernatural that had happened – and to me.

Although the recovery process still took a little time, it was soon clear that the Guillain-Barré syndrome had been checked. The paralysis receded and, by the time I was back to full strength, my consultant insisted that mine had been the quickest recovery from the condition on record.

I believe – we all believe – that God had miraculously healed me. And one thing was for sure: he now had my full attention.

3: Breaking In

_____

Above all, you must understand that no prophecy of Scripture
came about by the prophet's own interpretation of things.
For prophecy never had its origin in the human will.

2 Peter 1:20–21

In time, everything got back on its feet. We had another daughter, Lois, in April 1987, and moved into a huge, ramshackle, seven-bedroom terraced house in Sheringham, which we ran as a bed and breakfast while we renovated it, almost brick by brick.

Meanwhile, my work at The Grange had continued to confirm the convictions that had been forming in my mind since long before: that it is far better to raise children in a loving family environment than in an institution. There was one terrible example of this that convinced me beyond any doubt.

In spite of eight years' service at The Grange, I had been passed over for a promotion there to become senior residential social worker. I was pretty sore about this as I had felt, once again, that I had the future pretty well mapped out for myself. God, it seemed, had other plans, and I had to step sideways in my career when Norfolk County Council offered me a post at a therapeutic home for adolescents in Norwich. It was there that I came across a young lad called Gary.

Gary was a likeable rogue who had ended up in the home, but he hated it with a passion. He would do all he could to get away from it. Every summer he would get part-time work at the local fairground, run by members of the traveller community. He called them 'diddakois' – or 'dids' for short – but he meant the term affectionately. He loved them and they loved him and even wanted to foster him, but his social worker blocked that, doubtless with good reason: to the technocrat's mind, traveller families didn't offer secure homes, and there was (and still is) a lot of prejudice against them. In hindsight, this denial was probably a mistake. It should have been worth the risk.

One hot summer, Gary left the home for the last time, aged seventeen.

A few months later, on Christmas Eve, I received a phone call. Gary had put a brick through a Marks & Spencer shop-front window. The police had arrested him and he was in a cell in Norwich police station. I sighed, grabbed my coat and drove over.

To my surprise, when I got to his cell I found him quite cheerful.

'What *were* you thinking?' I asked him, sinking wearily into the chair opposite him.

He explained that after he had left the home, he had ended up living in an old car. He barely had any food, and most days he was freezing cold. 'At least in prison it's warm. And there's TV.' He seemed genuinely delighted about this. 'I heard on Christmas Day I'll get a turkey dinner, and even a beer! Besides,' he added, 'all my mates are in prison already.'

I shook my head in disbelief. 'Come off it, Gary. I've known you for years. You've been longing to get out of an institution all your life, and now here you are trying to break into one. What's going on?'

But as far as he was concerned, his decision made perfect sense. And even I could see that, from his point of view, there was a depressing logic to it. But it broke my heart. Despite his loathing for the children's home, the sad truth was that the place where Gary felt safest and most secure was inside an institution, even if that institution was a prison. And he wasn't alone. Those boys who went from care homes more or less directly into prison were all part of the same criminal subculture. For them, it was the only family they knew.

Two years later, Gary was found dead on the streets of Norwich. He simply wasn't able to survive in any normal community . . . and I knew we had failed him. So on the one hand, we had the problem of institutionalisation. On the other, we had the problem of moral corruption, if I can call it that.

There was another lad in the children's home called Eddie. He came in at the age of ten, having witnessed his father have a heart attack and die in front of him. His mother couldn't cope. She lost her grip on life and couldn't care for Eddie and he was brought into the home. He arrived bitter and angry, but I could tell immediately that there was something special about him. He had principles, and it was clear that, up until then, his parents had raised him well. I think the other children sensed it too and respected him for it, because he soon became a sort of kingpin in the home. But, influenced by everything else going on around him, he soon succumbed to the path, first of smoking, then of drinking and stealing.

Eddie had so much potential when he arrived, but within a few short years the institution turned him into someone he simply should never have become. He ended up going to prison for beating up some Eastern European lads who had allegedly molested a local Norfolk girl. The courts threw the book at him. Even so, having served half his time in prison, he was offered the opportunity to leave eighteen months early, on the condition that he didn't go back to Norwich where the incident had occurred. But Norwich was where all he knew and cared about were – his mother and friends – so he elected to serve the extra time rather than accept their condition.

Another strange choice, but I was learning how to put myself in the shoes of youngsters like Gary and Eddie and to understand their choices. I found that was the key to gaining their trust. The more I did that, the more I found I could encourage them in a positive direction, and so the more effective I became.

The first case where I really pushed back against the trend towards these negative outcomes looked, at least on the face of it, to be completely hopeless. There was a family of four boys whose father ruled them with a rod of iron, using fear to control them – or at least he tried to, until he gave up and abandoned both them and their mother. By then, she was close to breakdown. The four boys – aged between eight and fourteen – were, to all intents and purposes, feral: living off the streets, not going to school, involved in petty crime and misdemeanours. Whenever the police or social workers went to their home, the boys would flee like a pack of wolves. They said the youngest boy slept with one of their many dogs and, even at the age of eight, would only communicate with barks and growls. The family had stripped the house of all wood and burned it to heat the place. In the kitchen, when the social services were finally able to get in there, they found a dead dog decomposing, its carcass heaving with flies and maggots.

The obvious decision seemed to be to round up the boys and put them into care. But I wasn't happy with that choice. I was sure there must be another way. The father had vanished, but the mother still loved her boys. What she didn't need was the punishment of having them taken away from her. What she needed was encouragement and help – and plenty of both.

There was an empty council house close to where they were living and we moved the mother and the boys into that. We then recruited a whole social work team to support them. They helped the mother to get a haircut and some new clothes. She received counselling. The staff got to know the boys, figured out what they liked doing and found hobbies that matched their interests. We coached them into going back to school.

At a very basic level, we were remodelling their family. We taught the boys to respect their mother, which encouraged her and enabled her to feel strong enough to look after them. Within six months, we had found a new home for them all and they were able to start a new life together, this time on a firm footing.

The case was reckoned a complete success and marked the beginning of a new approach within the local social services – that if there was any way to keep the family unit together, then we had to do all we could to make that happen.

It was thanks to this case that I was appointed to the role of fostering officer for Norwich, even though I didn't have the necessary qualifications for the position. But they felt my experience meant I was a good fit for the job, and I would be able to study part-time at the University of East Anglia to augment my diploma into a full degree.

So I was thriving in my work and seemingly in my family too. Meanwhile, Liz had given birth to our third daughter, Megan. But, unnoticed by me, the cares and pressures of raising three little girls while I was distracted with work were becoming overwhelming. She was lonely, disillusioned and confused about life, drowning under the weight of cooking and cleaning and changing nappies.

With a husband who wasn't paying her the attention she deserved, why wouldn't Liz start wondering if this was all there was to life? But the question took her, at first, in an unexpected direction.

There were two Jehovah's Witnesses who lived on our street. One was a divorced woman living with her three sons; the other was a woman who had a little boy the same age as Rachel and an older daughter who loved helping Liz with baby Megan. As Liz started to get to know them as neighbours, they both invited her to join their study group. Her curiosity piqued, she decided to go along.

They were perfectly kind to her, and naturally enough took their opportunity to explain to Liz the core beliefs of Jehovah's Witnesses – about 'Jehovah God' and living on earth for ever – presumably hoping to convince her. Of course, when she told me about them and what she was doing, I wasn't at all happy about it, but I knew that if I tried to stop her, based on doubts that I couldn't have articulated at the time, it would only make her more determined to keep going. So I kept my concerns to myself and did what too many loved ones do in similar situations: absolutely nothing.

Meanwhile, her quest for answers, at least in that direction, seemed to bring Liz far more confusion than peace. She started sleeping badly, waking in the night with bouts of anxiety. Although she didn't talk much about the turmoil in her head, I knew there was something wrong, but I had no idea how to help.

Although I would say I had become a Christian as a young boy, through adolescence and early adulthood my church attendance had been sporadic. We had started attending the little Anglican church at the bottom of our road, and even the vicar become concerned about Liz's involvement with these Jehovah's Witnesses. This was exactly what the two women had told her would happen. 'They won't like that you're talking to us,' they warned her, 'but they're hypocrites. They'll try to keep you from knowing the true God.'

The pressures from each side started to weigh heavily on Liz. As well as her sense of disillusionment with life, she felt like all these different voices were arguing over the top of her head about what she should be doing. In the end, one day she found herself praying in exasperation, 'I can't listen to another person, God. Jesus, if you're real – because I know it's about you – can you show me?'

And then she opened up her Bible. The page fell open at the second letter of Peter in the New Testament, and her eye fell on this verse: 'Above all, you must understand . . .' She gasped, thinking to herself, 'I've found the most important verse in the whole Bible.' '. . . no prophecy of Scripture came about by the prophet's own interpretation of things.'

These words may mean little enough to you or me, or to anyone at the time. But for Liz, in that moment, this was her answer. Reading those words, she knew in her heart of hearts that what the Jehovah's Witnesses were preaching was the will of human beings, not the will of God. She knew without question.

'It wouldn't matter if the Pope had walked in and told me that I wasn't right,' she later told me. 'In that moment, I knew that I knew that I knew . . . that Jesus was the Son of God and the Jehovah's Witnesses were teaching a wrong gospel.'

Immediately she ran to our two neighbours and showed them

what she had found. 'Look at this scripture. This means you're wrong.'

But they only stared at her in bewilderment and said, 'But that verse doesn't mean anything of the sort to us.'

Leaving them unconvinced, she next called our Anglican vicar and told him how she knew that Jesus is real.

The vicar answered in his typically phlegmatic manner, 'Why, that's wonderful, Liz. Where was that scripture, you say?'

She barely waited to give him an answer, but instead shot off to some other neighbours – Margaret and Henry Upton – who lived on our street whom she knew to be Christians. She was hardly in the door before she was blurting out, 'The Jehovah's Witnesses are wrong! Jesus is real! It's all true!'

It was *that* sort of conversion, sudden and startling. She understood; she had clarity, like a light breaking in – a blast of revelation from above. As far as Liz was concerned, she had found the truth, so why wouldn't she tell it to everyone she knew?

Delighted by the unexpected intrusion, our elderly Christian neighbours answered with a joyful 'Praise the Lord!' They then explained that they had moved into the neighbourhood because God had told them to pray for people up and down that street. So they had bought that house and moved there *solely* with the purpose of praying for people. Following this encounter, Margaret invited Liz to join their Christian Bible study group.

As for me, I left for work that morning saying goodbye to one wife and was greeted that evening by an entirely different woman. I'm not sure, at first, she was exactly to my liking. It wasn't as if Liz had suddenly become an expert on the ins and outs of the Bible. But she had no qualms about nagging me about God. She'd say things like, 'You can't continue to live your life so distant from God,' or, 'You need to come back to God,' and, 'Do you even know how much God wants you?' In the evening, I'd go to put my arm around her and she would shove me away and say, 'Get off, I'm reading my Bible!' It was quite exhausting.

Liz would set little God-traps for me, she now admits, such as queuing up cassettes with Christian worship music in the car so that when I'd turn on the ignition in the morning and set off for work, I'd have some trendy worship leader warbling some awful tinny tune about Jesus at me.

Everything seemed to have divine significance to her. On one occasion, she picked up her Bible and started leaping about in excitement. 'It's hot, Robert! Look, my Bible's boiling hot! What do you think it means?'

I'm afraid I lost my temper. 'It's hot because I just took it off the TV, woman! Why don't you go and dig a hole in the garden and you can bury you and your stupid book right in it?!'

Nothing daunted, her response was to open her Bible, and then her eyes grew round as footballs. 'Look at this,' she cried. 'It says here, "And then they went and sat in holes in the ground." Holes in the ground! That's amazing!'

'Oh, now you're really going over the top, you are,' I growled in despair.

Those were some of the low points, I guess. But gradually I came to accept the change in my wife, and I couldn't deny the new radiance that shone out of her. She had never seemed more alive. Her new-found joy was infectious, and her confusion and anxiety were things of the past.

It didn't take her long to drag me along to the Uptons' Bible study group, and soon after that to the church they attended, called the Cromer Christian Fellowship. Whatever religion I had at the time was very definitely 'Church of England', so these groups and services, with their more charismatic flavour, made me feel deeply uncomfortable. Having said that, Henry Upton was ex-Navy, so we had a fair bit in common. And I soon began to see the difference that faith was making in these people's lives. They seemed good people, and we were beginning to find a real community with the other young families in the church.

I remember the change in one man in particular had a profound impact on me. Roger and Bryony lived a few doors down from us. Roger was an entrepreneur, a worldly type, and always short on time. It seemed his business wasn't doing well, and then we heard one day that he had lost everything overnight. One night, he got down on his knees in his kitchen and cried out to God, and God met him in a powerful way, so he said. He was a changed man. In one stroke he went from being angry and aggressive to the most smiling man I knew. I had never seen anything like that turnaround in someone's character before. And while, privately, I might have considered some of the more charismatic aspects of the church we were attending over-emotional or even credulous, I couldn't deny that change in Roger.

But while all this was going on, I had my own growing sense of restlessness. There were aspects of our life in Norfolk that I wanted to escape. I suppose I felt claustrophobic, hemmed in by family or the long, flat horizons. Or maybe it was my father's blood coursing through my veins: a question that needed an answer. A call to adventure.

One night I turned to Liz in bed. 'So are we going to stay in Norfolk for the rest of our lives?' I asked.

'I don't know. Do you *want* to go somewhere else?'

'Maybe . . .' I answered. '. . . Yes.'

I just had no idea where.

4: Preparation

Commit to the LORD whatever you do,
and he will establish your plans.
(Proverbs 16:3)

It was out of this restlessness that I applied for a position as a fostering officer on Guernsey, one of the English Channel Islands, located to the north-west of France. It's about as far away from Norfolk as you can get and still be in the British Isles.

I knew there had been a lot of applicants for the job so I was taken aback when they selected me for the first round of interviews in London, and downright shocked when I made the shortlist of four to travel to Guernsey for the final assessment. Knowing the other applicants on the list, I realised my chances of getting the job were next to zero – each one of them was far more qualified than me. And so, thinking it might be the only opportunity we would ever have to visit the island, I invited Liz along. Baby Anna, our fourth and latest daughter born in February 1991, also came with us, riding on Liz's hip.

It was November and, to be frank, the island was grim. We were staying on the southern coast, looking out over the vast expanse of the Atlantic Ocean, and it was bleak beyond description. Cold, wet and dark, girt with black, forbidding cliffs smashed by rough seas. Not exactly the picturesque idyll that Liz had been expecting. I told her she didn't need to worry: we would never have to live there, since one of the other better-qualified applicants was sure to get the job.

But I was wrong about that.

After the interview, we were asked to wait for a couple of hours on the island and then call a number to get the final decision.

'We want to offer you the job,' said the lady who had interviewed me.

I nearly dropped the phone. 'That's very kind of you,' I said, once I'd recovered from the shock, 'but to be brutally honest, I can't see how it's going to work with my wife and four children – financially, I mean.'

'Yes, we had thought of that. That's why we'd like to offer you a salary two grades higher than the one advertised. How does that sound?'

Too good to refuse, was the answer.

We arrived as a family of six in the spring of 1992 and found a paradise awaiting us. Gone were the brooding rocks and the stormy seas; they had been replaced with balmy beaches of white sand stretching for miles, with hidden coves and aquamarine waters. To Liz and me, it felt like we were on a permanent holiday. You could buy fresh produce on the roadside. The banks and heaths and meadows were a carpet of wild flowers.

It was an idyllic place to raise our four girls. I always started work early so I could be home by 4.30 p.m., and in summer we would head straight for the beach and spend the rest of the day there, having picnic suppers and mucking about in the surf and the rock pools.

We lived in a farmhouse called Les Martin in the parish of St Martin, which stood on a hill with a stream running through the garden. Behind the house there was a narrow, winding road that led down to a secluded beach called Petit Bot Bay. We kept forty chickens on the property and every morning the girls would collect whatever eggs they could find, wash them, box them and sell them on the roadside. Any money they made they got to keep as pocket money.

I couldn't have dreamed of a life like that. I sometimes found myself wondering what we had done to deserve it all. But now, looking back, I can see how important our years on Guernsey were for us as a family. They were the preparation ground, a breathing space, a time of bonding and of establishing our values, of defining who we were as a family before all that was to come.

You'd think four daughters would have been enough of a handful, and I was quite satisfied with the size of our family. But one day we had a visit from Jonathan, the pastor of the church we were attending on the island.

'I had a dream that you were holding a little blond boy,' he told Liz, 'and he was your baby.'

Liz raised her eyebrows at me. I confess the idea threw me, but I wanted to be faithful and I knew that Liz had always wanted to have a little boy, so I told her we would try for one month. 'One last chance. If you don't become pregnant, then that's it . . .'

The result? Twin boys, of course.

It was a shock, and I have to admit that when I heard the news from the doctor my first thought was, 'What car are we going to get?' I didn't even know if they made cars that could fit a family of eight.

Nine months later, on 14 June 1993, our pastor's dream proved at least partly true. Not one, but two healthy baby boys: Joel Isaac and Joshua Samuel. Our family was now complete.

Professionally, I was settling into my role working for the Guernsey Children's Board. I started out as its fostering officer but over time I was promoted and promoted, and within a few years I was running the whole suite of adolescent services. This meant everything from residential care, through fostering and adoption, to responsibility for the secure unit – an alternative to prison for young offenders. All of this confirmed what I had learned in Norfolk: that the best way to raise any child, but particularly an adolescent, was in a secure family environment, preferably their own natural one, and not within an institution. So that became my goal, to move children out of institutions and into families, and, as a ruling passion, it would soon come to define our life's work in China. As you'll see, God began to pave the route that would eventually lead our family out there.

> *And afterwards,*
> *I will pour out my Spirit on all people.*
> *Your sons and daughters will prophesy,*
> *your old men will dream dreams,*
> *your young men will see visions.*
> (Joel 2:28)

The early 1990s were an exceptional time in the Church around the world. It began with a phenomenon that came to be known as the Toronto Blessing, although in fact what began in the city of Toronto in January 1994 was also going on elsewhere around the world. In China, South America and Africa, it seemed that God was pouring out his Holy Spirit in a new and powerful way, beginning with charismatic Christian communities but quickly spreading even into quite conservative churches too, including the Catholic Church.

Worshipping communities began to experience manifestations of the Holy Spirit similar to those they had only ever read about in the book of Acts in the New Testament: the Spirit coming as a wind or a holy fire. People physically touched by the presence of God were being shaken or falling down. There was a widespread gift of speaking in tongues across all manner of denominations; the gifts of prophecy and healing miracles became common occurrences, with extraordinary reports circulating like wildfire between believing communities of all nations. And many new believers came into the Church. Revival appeared to be breaking out across the world.

On Guernsey, we had settled into a moderate congregation of about a hundred people, full of young families like ours. It was called King's Church in St Peter Port and was run by a gifted teacher in his late twenties called Jonathan Le Tocq. In late 1993 – so still a short while before the so-called Toronto Blessing took

off – we heard that a man called David Devenish would be coming
to speak at King's. David was a pastor from a family of churches
called New Frontiers and had an acknowledged prophetic ministry.
Personally, I was still sceptical of such 'gifts' that purported to be
supernatural, but I was also more than a little nervous about what
he might say.

So on the day he came to speak, I made sure I was sitting way
at the back of the church. I planned to watch and observe what
happened, and at the same time was hoping he wouldn't come
anywhere near me. He spoke eloquently and then afterwards
offered to pray for people in the congregation. As he moved
among the other people, he suddenly caught my eye at the back
and walked straight through the crowd towards me. I was a little
taken aback, but I let him pray for me.

'I sense you are going to be a father to as many children as
there are stars in the sky,' he said in a quiet voice beside me.

Having declared this over me, he moved on. I was left thinking,
'That's interesting, but also quite strange.' We had six children
and that was quite enough for me.

After the service, Liz and I discussed what David had said. She
thought maybe it referred to my involvement in the youth group
and Sunday school. But you could hardly consider those a multitude. Nonplussed, I put David's prophetic word to the back of
my mind.

But this wouldn't be the last time I heard those exact same
words: *a father to as many children as there are stars in the sky.*

A few months after this encounter the outworking of the Toronto
Blessing really started to be felt across various church networks
in the UK. Each summer since we had arrived in Guernsey, we
had been taking the children to a week-long event called Stoneleigh
Bible Week, organised by the New Frontiers family of churches
and held on a huge agricultural showground south of Coventry.
It ran for ten years in all, and by its conclusion the number of
attendees had climbed to something like twenty-six thousand

people. The week would consist of worship sessions and a lot of good, solid teaching, as well as being a great time of bonding for us as a family and of forging many lasting Christian friendships.

It was at Stoneleigh in 1994 that we started seeing more-dramatic manifestations of the Holy Spirit in the big worship meetings. People were falling over – what is called being 'slain in the Spirit' – and weeping and laughing. Others were declaring words of knowledge and prophecy over each other, and yet others described visions they had seen while being prayed for. The church leaders said it was like it had happened in the book of Acts when the Holy Spirit came upon the disciples on the day of Pentecost. Seeing it for myself, I still found the whole thing pretty uncomfortable.

'They're being pushed over,' said one of the other men we knew one evening, with a wry chuckle. 'They must be.' I think he was only half joking, since all of it was far outside the limits of our experience (not to mention our comfort zones). I certainly wasn't up for anyone pushing me over. It had to be real or I didn't want it.

When we all returned to Guernsey, our little church started a series of Saturday evening services we called The Filling Station. People came from all over the island, hungry to experience more of God. We went along most Saturdays, and at one service someone came up to pray for me. As he was praying, he said, 'The Holy Spirit is gentle. He won't impose on you, but you are grieving him by holding out on him. If you want to experience the Holy Spirit, you must stop resisting him.'

As he said that, I felt it cut to my heart. I knew he was right. I had been holding out. I'd built myself a wall and was hiding behind it, perhaps fearful of where it might lead if I were to let God in fully.

'Lord, forgive me,' I prayed. 'I don't understand all this, but I am going to let go. Your will be done, not mine.' I had hardly murmured those words when I fell suddenly to the ground, and there I stayed for a long time, experiencing what felt like wave after wave of peace flowing through my body. It was awesome in the truest sense of awe. I felt so full of the love of God, and yet, at the same time, I was convicted of having judged others' experiences of him, of having doubted them.

It was a powerful rupture of the wall I had built up.

The strange thing was, I realised it was a phenomenon of which I already had some memory. As a child, accompanying my mother to church, often when it came time to go forward for Communion, I would have what my mother called a 'fainting episode'. This happened on many occasions, although only at Communion, and despite the fact that I never fainted at any other time in my life. No one at the time recognised it for what I now know it to be. I remember the vicar used to say, when I came round, 'Just give the boy a nice cup of tea . . . P-p-put in plenty of sugar, too.'

Maybe God had had his hand on me for longer than I knew.

A few weeks later, I was at one of these Filling Station meetings, my eyes closed, praying . . . staring into space. In that space, I suddenly saw Jesus on the cross. He was looking straight at me. And then, as I looked, he came down off the cross, walked towards me and folded his arms around me.

There was something in that act of love that was so profound, so powerful, that I started sobbing uncontrollably. I'd always thought of myself as a man's man (whatever that means). I was good at keeping it together. Now, in front of everyone, I wept like a child, completely broken, while the pain of being fatherless was touched by God's hand. Not healed – not then – but opened up. Acknowledged. He knew the secret pain that was hidden in my heart.

God was humbling me at the same time as he was getting my whole heart. In those moments, I was discovering the true heart of the Father, the Everlasting Father who loves us through his own Son. I was also discovering the freedom that came with trusting God completely, with my whole heart. There was no doubt in my mind now: the Holy Spirit was real. I was encountering the God who speaks, the Eternal God who is the same yesterday, today and tomorrow. I wanted to give my whole life to him then, to keep nothing back, to turn it all over into his hands.

In the days that followed, Liz and I often prayed together, voicing that same desire: that God would use the whole of our lives to serve him to whatever ends he saw fit.

Jesus was our Lord.

And we resolved to be obedient to whatever he asked of us.

5: China Calling

The LORD had said to Abram, 'Go from your country, your people and your father's household to the land I will show you.'
(Genesis 12:1)

Guernsey was a good place for us. My career was heading in the right direction; I was growing into a role of some influence on the island, at least in the area of social services. It was a wonderful place to raise a large family. We were seeing young people's lives changed through our outreach work for the church, and our own faith was growing and maturing. And yet, for all that, I was again becoming increasingly restless. The small seed of desire to go to China one day, although it had been dormant for some time, had never died, and now it started showing signs of new life.

On the face of it, the desire was far less practical than ever before. We had six children now. Even if an opportunity ever were to arise, the challenge of relocating as a family of eight seemed immense. Liz was very patient whenever I revisited this old idea.

One day I saw a job advertised in Hong Kong and thought that at last this was my chance. We agreed I should go for it, and so I applied. But, in spite of my high hopes, I didn't get it. I was crushed.

'Never mind,' said Liz, trying to make me feel better. 'We're happy in Guernsey anyway. God must want something else for you – at least for now.'

I tried to let it go. But there was something about China that I couldn't shake off.

Even at this stage, I hadn't made the connection between what I was doing and my heart for China. I imagined, if I were to get out there at all, that it would be as an evangelist or a preacher, working in support of the underground church.

It was around this time that I read a couple of books about an English missionary to China in the mid- to late nineteenth century, a Yorkshireman called James Hudson Taylor. Reading about his extraordinary courage and zeal for the gospel, in what was then still a very alien culture for an Englishman, fired my imagination. Hudson Taylor became a bit of a hero to me.

I came across other books as well. One was called *Lilies Amongst Thorns* by Brother Danyun and was full of extraordinary stories about the more recent growth of the Chinese Church under Communism. It showed, really beyond doubt, that the persecution of Christians went hand in hand with revival. Or vice versa. Then there was Jackie Pullinger's book, *Chasing the Dragon*, an amazing tale of a young woman following God's call to hop on a boat heading for the Far East. Hardly knowing her final destination, she ended up ministering to some of the toughest criminals in Asia in the infamous Walled City in Hong Kong.

These were the sorts of adventures, I suppose, that I had in mind. Yet how was that practical with a family of eight?

In a sense, I was looking down the wrong end of the telescope. I wasn't a preaching evangelist, but what I did have by then was nearly twenty years of experience in social work. You might think it would have occurred to me that, if God wanted to use me in China, it would have something to do with that. But it never did.

That summer at Stoneleigh, Terry Virgo, who led the event, asked me to act as bag-carrier for a visiting speaker called Dennis Balcombe. At the time, Dennis was quite well known for his work in Hong Kong and further afield around Asia. He had started a church on the island in 1969 which, after some initial opposition, flourished, and he soon became known for his support of the house churches on the mainland.

I was asked to show Dennis around Stoneleigh, generally make him feel welcome, show him his room, explain his schedule, that sort of thing. Of course, doing this, I got to hear straight from the horse's mouth about his heart for China and all the work he'd been doing for more than two decades by then. What I couldn't get over was why Terry Virgo had chosen me to look after Dennis. As far as Terry was concerned, we were just an ordinary family attending the week. No one except Liz and my children, and maybe a friend or two, knew of my passion for China, and certainly not Terry, so it amazed me that, out of the blue, he had picked me.

I'd love to say that meeting Dennis was the inspiration that triggered everything that followed, but that's not exactly how it happened. What it did do, after our lengthy conversations, was cause me to dig deeper into my interest in the country. I started doing more and more research, not just about the house churches there, but about the country in general, with one eye open on how I might fit in.

What caught my attention the most was China's one-child policy. Although as a concept it's relatively well known, it's worth explaining exactly what this was. It was first implemented in 1979 as part of a generalised birth planning programme designed to control the size of China's rapidly expanding population by placing a limit on the number of births parents could have. It subsequently underwent various modifications. For example, in the mid-1980s it was decided that parents living in rural communities were allowed a second child if their first had been a daughter. There were a few other exceptions, such as if the parents were of a certain ethnic minority group. In fact, 'one-child' was a bit of a misnomer, since for most of the policy's lifespan, a small percentage of parents in China were allowed a second child.

Nevertheless, the policy had a marked effect on the population and its behaviour in connection with children. In rural areas especially, families were often reliant on their sons to provide for them in old age. Daughters, if they married, had to help care for their husband's parents, not their own. Thus, China's orphanages began to fill up with healthy girls and disabled boys. Many parents decided that, if they could only have one child, it needed to be a healthy boy.

The more I found out about the orphanages in China, the more I realised these were institutions in crisis. The burgeoning numbers were so large that it was becoming a huge challenge for the Chinese government to find the necessary resources to care for the nation's orphans. Only then did I begin to see an area where I believed I could help. Nowhere in all my research did I find any mention of fostering programmes. It seemed an entirely unknown concept in China at that time. But all my experience of working with children, and especially adolescents, in England told me that the best outcome for the orphans would be to be placed within loving substitute families. This would have the added benefit of relieving the incredible pressures on the orphanage institutions themselves.

So I started to see a path for me. For us.

Later that year, I heard about a research grant that was available for social workers to undertake a project in a developing country. I decided to apply to see if I could get the funding I would need to go to China to investigate alternatives to institutional care for orphans. I felt the application was strong, but again I was disappointed.

'They're looking for young academics,' I moaned, rather bitterly, to Liz, 'not some ageing social worker from Guernsey.'

'Ageing? You're not even forty!' she replied.

I knew I had to snap out of my funk, even as I saw another door to China close.

The following summer, in July 1996, I went to the first few days of Stoneleigh alone. (Liz and I had decided that bringing all six children for the whole week was too much, so she would arrive halfway through the conference and I would return to Guernsey to take over with the children.)

I spent my days at Stoneleigh helping out with the youth ministry. After one morning meeting, a stranger came up to me and asked if he could pray for me. From his accent, I could tell he was Australian. 'Sure,' I said, 'if you like,' not thinking much of it.

He started praying, at first a few things I don't remember, but then he said, 'I feel God is saying that within this year you are going to be in an earthquake. Where this happens is where God wants you to be.'

'That's pretty specific,' I thought to myself, nodding along agreeably, but reflecting that it was a word I should probably hold lightly.

When I mentioned to my pastor friend Jonathan later that evening what had happened, he joked, 'Well, that's Aussies for you. He probably doesn't even know we don't get earthquakes in this country.'

I laughed and thought nothing more of it. But I guess God was laughing louder than either of us . . .

The next day, I left the conference as Liz arrived. That evening she went along to the main meeting where a man called forward for prayer anyone who felt called to go to other nations.

'What a shame Robert's not here,' Liz thought to herself, but then decided to go forward on my behalf. A woman came to pray with her.

'Where do you feel called to?' the woman asked.

'Oh, it's not me!' Liz laughed. 'It's my husband. He feels called to China.'

The lady gave Liz a knowing smile and then turned her attention to prayer. Afterwards, Liz thanked her and was about to leave when the lady caught her elbow. 'Let me know when *you* get to China,' she said with a glint in her eye.

It was only then that the penny dropped. Up till then, it hadn't really sunk in that if I were called to China, then that meant her as well, and our children.

'I've been had,' she thought, as she walked away. But she was determined to be faithful. She decided there and then that she would share my dream and go with me, even if she didn't want to.

All this prayer was well and good, but the fact was that our life was in Guernsey and not China. I hadn't even been there and still had no idea how I was going to get there.

It was at this point that a friend in the church, James McIlwraith, stepped into the breach. James had been in the cider business before he had sold his company in Devon and moved to Guernsey. He later returned to Devon to run a dairy farm. His little cider company had been the beneficiary of a price war between Bulmers and Gaymers; one of them (I forget which) had bought him and his brother-in-law out of their 4-per-cent share of the cider market for a considerable sum of money.

James and I were having a chat over a pint one evening when I mentioned my growing interest in helping orphans in China.

'So,' he shrugged, 'let's go.'

'What?'

'Let's go to China. I've got a bit of spare cash knocking around.' I knew that was an understatement. 'I'll pay. You pray,' he chuckled. 'Besides, I've always wanted to see the Terracotta Army . . .'

It was a mightily generous offer. But he was absolutely serious.

At last, I was going to China.

6: The Earth Thunders

*Suddenly there was such a violent earthquake that the foundations
of the prison were shaken. At once all the prison doors flew open,
and everyone's chains came loose.*

(Acts 16:26)

The aerial approach into Kai Tak Airport would be a thrilling
arrival for anyone coming East for the first time, plunging down
as it does onto the short runway that juts out into Hong Kong
harbour like a jagged tooth while washing-lines draped with
Chinese laundry whip past your window. But for me, the adren-
aline didn't stop there. This was it. After all those years of thinking
about it, I was finally here.

It was November 1996 – a beautiful time of year to visit Hong
Kong when, for a few blessed weeks, the smog drifting down
from the mainland factories clears and the humidity cools into
long, bright days of azure skies that melt away into coral sunsets
and balmy neon-lit nights.

This was adventure, at last.

This wasn't to say that the trip was unplanned. On the contrary,
James and I had worked hard to arrange an itinerary that encom-
passed several cities out of the vastness of China. We had written
to ask Dennis Balcombe if we could drop in on him. And to
Jackie Pullinger, whose solo ministry to the Triad gangs that
controlled the Walled City (in Kowloon) was renowned around
the global Church. As I mentioned, her book *Chasing the Dragon*
had been fuel to the fire of my desire to come to China. At the
time of our visit, the Walled City had only fairly recently been
demolished (in December 1993) to make way for a more whole-
some recreational park. But Jackie's ministry to the poorest gangs

in Hong Kong had continued unabated, and we were keen to visit her.

Besides these two, we had arranged to meet a young man called David Gotts who was working in an orphanage in the city of Changsha in the central province of Hunan. After that we would fly to Shanghai and then west to another contact, Elizabeth Middleton, in Xi'an, the ancient city that sits at the eastern terminus of the Silk Road where James would at last get to see his beloved Terracotta Army. The last city on our itinerary was Beijing.

The trip was immersive from the start.

We visited Jackie Pullinger at what I now think of as her 'old place', a small collection of Nissen huts located in the hills of the New Territories north of Hong Kong island. We attended one of her meetings and were immediately struck by the make-up of her congregation. It was a long way from the family atmosphere of Stoneleigh and the other churches I was used to. She had a group of fifty or sixty, mostly men, who were covered in tattoos and scars, some with fingers and teeth missing. These were tough guys, ex-Triads for the most part, but they were worshipping with an intensity I'd never witnessed before.

The noise when we entered the room was terrific. And that was before Jackie made her entrance. In she came, and from one moment to the next, you could have heard a pin drop. All these tough ex-criminals had such love and respect for her. She moved among them, nodding at one, reaching out and grasping the hand of another, murmuring greetings softly left and right. And then she stood and glared at them all from the front. 'Right,' she said, lifting her voice, 'now we are really going to worship. You all dance in the bars and dance in the nightclubs, don't you? Well, now you're going to dance for Jesus.'

And boy, did they!

Instantly, this felt like a different world to me. And after the worship, I sat outside in the autumn sunshine with two guys who could speak some English. We stayed there for some time as they shared their lives, telling me what they had been through. Each had a remarkable story, but in another sense their stories were typical of every one of the young men who were coming to those meetings. Each had a story of how their life had been turned around by Jesus, many of them set free from drugs and other forms of addiction.

'I've just been watching you with those guys,' said a voice behind me when we were done talking. It was Jackie.

'They're good men,' I replied.

'That's what they need, you know. Someone like you to talk to.'

'Well, you must get loads of visitors–'

'Not like you,' she said, cutting me off. 'Oh, we get visitors, sure. Mostly they're younger men or women. But no father figures. That's what these men need – to be able to speak, one man to another, to a man older and wiser than them.'

Well, I knew that was true. Every young man needs that.

'Will you promise to come and visit whenever you're through Hong Kong? To come and talk with the boys?'

'Sure,' I shrugged, 'although I've no idea if I'll ever be back here.'

'You'll be back. And when you are, I'm going to hold you to your promise.' She smiled at me, while her eyes fixed me with that famous glare of hers, and I knew then that she would.

From Hong Kong, we crossed the mainland border into the urban sprawl of Guangzhou, where Dennis Balcombe had arranged for us to visit Pastor Lamb, another famous figure in the underground church.

It was here that it started to become clear that my travelling companion, James, would be no great fan of China. To be fair to China, James was no great fan of people in general. He was a Devon dairy farmer (and self-made millionaire) who didn't even much like animals – although he liked them slightly better than he liked people – who had been dropped into a land where there were more teeming millions of people than anywhere else on earth. The seas of heads we started to encounter, first at border crossings and then on public transport, started to raise his hackles.

The Chinese don't queue like the English; they huddle (as any visitor trying to get through Chinese passport control well knows). James had a suitcase with him that looked like a piece of military hardware, made entirely of metal, with big rivets, industrial clasps and very sharp corners. The thing must have weighed thirty kilos. When his patience in these 'huddles' was stretched to breaking point, he would sling down his mammoth suitcase in front of any particularly troublesome traveller and growl, 'Now you try pushing, eh?' Even with their bruised shins, I'm not sure the lesson was well learned, but at least it made James feel like he was giving back as good as he got.

There was more cultural friction to come in our hotel in Guangzhou. Pastor Lamb had arranged for us to stay in a modest place downtown. At breakfast time, James and I went downstairs to the basement dining hall ready to chance our luck with our first proper mainland Chinese food. The ceiling of the room was unusually low, and the two of us cut rather hulking figures while we cast our gaze around for a free table. Of course, as soon as we entered, every Chinese person in the place stopped eating their breakfast and stared at us. We made quite the entrance, apparently.

We settled into our places and the waitress came over to take our order. With us not speaking any Mandarin, and she with no English, she went away and returned with a menu that had pictures of various breakfast choices on it. I pointed at one that looked like it would do the job, and she looked at me, her eyes staring in astonishment. '*Zhen de?*' she kept saying, which I took to mean, 'Really?'

I nodded away, unsure quite what her issue was, and so she turned to James.

'That'll do for me too,' he said, pointing to the same picture. Again, the same astonished expression. 'Yes, yes – two of those please.'

As she went away to pass on our order, we couldn't help noticing her drop a comment or two to the other guests on her way to the kitchen. Pretty soon there were more than a few glances in our direction, and it was obvious that several tables were talking about us. When, at last, our order arrived from the kitchen, several people appeared in the kitchen doorway, apparently to watch us eat our breakfast. By now, I was getting used to people looking at us merely because we were foreigners, but even this was a bit much.

All was made clear once the waitress started setting down our breakfast on the table in front of us. We had ordered breakfast for ten. Each. So there we were with breakfast for twenty squeezed onto our little table, with dozens of Chinese diners now looking on in admiration and not a little wonder. As far as Sino–British cultural relations went, I suppose we must have left them as confused as ever.

From Guangzhou, we returned by rail to Hong Kong, and the following day we took a short flight north to Changsha, a city famous for being Mao's birthplace and home town. An acquaint-ance Ross Patterson, a long-serving missionary in Asia, had put me in touch with David Gotts, who was still only nineteen and working in an orphanage there.

David had booked us in to a local hotel, although it was a notch or two down from what we had experienced so far. The room stank of sewage, thanks to a drainage system not unlike a medi-eval castle. The toilets for every room on our floor emptied into the same open gully that passed in through one wall of our 'ensuite' and out the other. So if we were in there brushing our teeth and we heard a flush from next door, a second or two later our neighbours' recent deposit would come floating through our bathroom. The fact that there were several rooms 'upstream' of us meant that there was pretty steady traffic.

We did our best to stem the stench by laying soaking towels along the bottom of the connecting door to the bedroom, but it really did little good. And it did even less for James's mood. After a fairly sleepless night on beds as hard as tables, we were awoken at five o'clock the next morning by speakers blaring out some sort of reveille at the local university. James dragged himself angrily out of bed and went to open the curtains to take a look. He was met with a grim view of steaming chimney stacks from the nearby factories and a thick, grey smog drifting over the broken tiles of the roofs below him.

'SHUT UP!' he bellowed at the city, to no effect whatsoever, and then turned back to me. 'Welcome to Slums-R-Us,' he muttered with a grimace.

Despite this none-too-salubrious start, the visit to the orphanage was destined to make a deep impression on me. This Cheshire lad, David, with his boyish features and white blond hair, had somehow ended up running a unit he had started himself within the orphanage, which specialised in care for disabled children. In the main orphanage there were several hundred children and babies – far more than the facility was designed for – with only a few overworked and untrained staff to look after them all. It was the staff, in fact, who struck me first. Seeing them, and how they lived and responded to the children, I realised that before any positive change could be made that would benefit the children, we had to do something for the staff. We had to give them some hope. They were overworked, overstretched and under-skilled. The staff needed training and a lot of encouragement.

As we were walking around the long, bleak corridors, we passed through a doorway and a young boy of six or seven came up to me and grabbed my hand. He was wearing shoes that were several sizes too big for him, and a grubby pair of shorts and a T-shirt. We had to move on, but this kid wouldn't let go of my hand. He wasn't crying or upset; he just didn't want me to go. As gently as I could, I prised my hand out of his, although it took some doing.

As I walked away, I was surprised how deeply the encounter affected me. In those few moments, that small boy represented to me all the abandoned and orphaned children of China, clinging on to hope. I vowed that, somehow, I would return to China to help children like him.

At this stage of the trip, James and I were having almost comically different experiences. James loathed China – at least what we had seen so far – with a deep and growing passion. After the Changsha hotel room, he was genuinely on the hunt for a British Airways office so he could get on a flight out of there. (Of course, he didn't have much luck in a place like Changsha.)

I, on the other hand, was in the grip of a sort of existential and spiritual high I've rarely known. Sure, there were some disasters on the trip, but, for me, the God experiences were so real. The best way I can think to describe it is this: from the moment of our arrival, it was as if we had stepped into a big mansion and were passing from room to room seeing different things, and God was going ahead of us, smoking a big cigar. Everywhere we went, I could sort of smell God's presence, like he had just been there and we were merely following a path he had already prepared for us. I had never experienced anything like that before. And in Shanghai, his aroma was about to get a lot stronger.

If we thought the cities we had visited before were populous, nothing could have prepared us for Shanghai. In all my life, I had never seen so many people in one place, even just arriving at the airport. It was quite overwhelming.

Of the five or six cities on our itinerary, Shanghai was the only one in which we hadn't managed to organise any contacts to visit. But that didn't bother me. I was just excited to be there. Shanghai was what it was all about for me. Part of the reason for this was that The Bund, a waterfront area in central Shanghai, was the original spot where my greatest hero in the faith, James Hudson Taylor, had landed on 1 March 1854.

Hudson Taylor went on to found the China Inland Mission and was responsible for bringing more than eight hundred missionaries to the country, which, in turn, saw a remarkable growth in Christianity there. He was said to have been personally responsible for more than eighteen thousand converts. If I had to name one man who had inspired my passion for China, it would be him. What I admired about him was his cultural sensitivity to the Chinese. He learned not only Mandarin and Cantonese, but also many regional dialects, and he soon dressed in Chinese clothes and even grew a long pigtail like many Chinese people wore at the time.

But it wasn't so much his outward assimilation of Chinese culture that I so admired, as his sincere desire to understand the minds and motives of Chinese people. He loved them deeply. And I was sure, if anyone was to do any good in China and carry any influence, that must be the right approach. At least, that would be my approach.

So, as we touched down in Shanghai, I was feeling excited and inspired. But effectively we knew no one in the city, we had no one to meet and we had nothing specific to do. God, on the other hand, had something very specific in mind for us, and he didn't waste his time making it happen.

Having recovered our luggage from an almighty scrum of people in the arrivals hall, we went outside into the street. The air was full of cries of 'Taxi! Taxi! You want taxi?!' Aside from the buses and cars, we were immediately accosted by dozens of people trying to sell us everything from hotels to tourist excursions. If James had had a big stick, I'm sure he would have started laying about him. His face was like thunder. But that didn't stop an enterprising young woman coming up to him and waving a pair of tickets in his face. 'Two tickets to Special Olympics Opening Ceremony,' she parroted with great enthusiasm. 'You want? Tickets free! No price!'

'Special Olympics? What?' he said, all in a fluster. 'No, we don't want your stupid tickets, woman. Clear off!'

'Hold on a second,' I said. The word 'Olympics' had triggered something in my mind. On the Sunday before we left, James and I had been prayed for by some of the other members of our church back in Guernsey. One young girl had declared a vision. She said she saw a picture of us carrying an Olympic torch into China. At the time, I thought little enough of it. There were no connections in my mind between China and the Olympics (this was long before China won the bid for the 2008 Summer Olympics). And I didn't even know there was such an event as the 'Special Olympics'. But as soon as I heard that word, I knew in my heart that this was from God.

'We'll take 'em,' I said, plucking them from her hand.

'What?' protested James. 'It's bound to be some scam.'

'What scam? They're free, for goodness sake! Come on,' I urged. 'Whatever it is, it could be fun.'

That same afternoon, having dumped our stuff in the Magnolia Hotel in the centre of Shanghai, we found ourselves picking our way up to our allocated seats high above the track in the most enormous stadium I had ever seen. I've since learned that whatever the event was that we attended, it couldn't have been the official international Special Olympics, even though that's what the lady had said. We think it was actually the *National* Special Olympics Opening Ceremony (in other words, including all the Paralympic track and field events, but all the competitors were Chinese). In any case, *something* very spectacular was going on, with thousands upon thousands of meticulously choreographed and uniformed performers filling the arena.

We were seated in a section full of delegates from across the Asia-Pacific region. Next to James was an Australian man who was the Chairman of Fosters Lager in China. With his cider-brewing background, James and he had plenty to talk about. On the other side, next to me, was a venerable old gentleman introduced to me as a senior member of the Communist Party. Straight away, I thought, 'Here we go. I'd better watch myself or this could be trouble.'

As we watched the impressive spectacle unfold below us, I listened to this old gentleman – whose English was very good – talk about the Cultural Revolution and how he had taught English in his early career but then had been forced to switch to Russian. I, in turn, told him about my work in social care with children back home in England. As soon as I mentioned working with children, his eyes lit up. It seemed that, in his retirement, he had become involved in a lot of charity work to do with children, specifically acting as a bridge between the local orphanage in Shanghai and foreigners who wanted to help in diverse ways or even adopt.

Out of the blue he suddenly declared, 'Of course, all the work I do for the children is for my Father,' and he glanced heavenward.

Call me a cynic, but my first thought was, 'Yeah, yeah. He's just trying to catch me out.' So I just nodded politely and kept schtum. He, meanwhile, started to talk about having grown up as a child in a Catholic mission school in the southern province of Yunnan. Before I knew it, I opened my mouth and out came the words, 'We're Christians and we've come to China with a heart to serve.'

I say 'out came the words' because I really wasn't thinking what I was saying. I just sort of blurted it out, and as I did so my heart started racing. The old gentleman – his English name was John (and he was married to Mary, so there was a clue!) – looked at me for a few moments, and then asked, 'Which hotel did you say you were staying in?'

'The Magnolia.'

He nodded like an old sage. 'I would like to invite you and your friend to lunch. I shall send a car for you tomorrow.' And then he gave me a time to be ready.

At once I thought, 'Oh, Lord, what have I done?' I had blown our cover wide open, and I couldn't figure out whether that was a good or a bad thing. But I couldn't say anything to James until after the event was over.

'What's up, Rob?' he asked as we were walking down the tunnel towards the exit. 'You look like you've got the weight of the world on your shoulders.'

I nodded and clenched my jaw. 'I think I did something stupid. You know the guy I was sitting next to?'

James shrugged. 'The Communist Party guy? What about him?'

'I told him we were Christians and now he's sending a car to pick us up in the morning. I think we could be in trouble.'

Needless to say, James wasn't overjoyed by this news.

But any worries we might have harboured that night couldn't have been more unfounded. The next day the car was there at the appointed hour and took us off to a restaurant where another event was already in progress. It seemed to be some sort of meeting between several western organisations and the local

Shanghai civil authorities on the subject of childcare. James and I were in the room, as it were, but no one was paying us much attention. We had no agenda, after all. Representatives from two well-known international NGOs that support children took their turns to give their presentations. Each talk sounded, to my ear, like a protracted exercise in finger-wagging, putting the blame on certain policies in place for the bad statistics in China's orphanage care. Even as new to the culture as I then was, I was pretty sure this wouldn't go down well with the local authorities, since no one appreciates being talked down to.

Meanwhile, James and I were enjoying the spread that had been laid on, which was quite a banquet. There were platters and platters of the most delicious food.

'I love your food,' I kept saying to our hosts, and, 'What lovely beer you have!' I didn't even know they made beer in China, but an ice-cold Tsingtao went down very nicely. Our Chinese hosts seemed delighted by my enthusiasm for their hospitality.

One of them, a certain Mr Shí (pronounced 'Shur'), asked me what I thought about what the foreign NGOs had said. Well, it wasn't for me to come all the way from the other side of the world and start criticising the Chinese on their own turf, so I started to explain my view that there were positive alternatives to institutions and orphanages, such as family care.

'What do you mean by that?' he asked.

I explained that it involved the long-term placement of orphans within families. (As far as I know, family placement was an unknown concept in China at the time.) I impressed on him how important I felt it was for a child to be raised in a family context if he or she were to flourish. The way I saw it, I said, as respectfully as I could, China's main problem with its orphanages was the sheer volume of children to be looked after, on the one hand; and on the other, that large swathes of their staff were untrained, unmotivated or else overwhelmed. Sometimes all three. Mr Shí nodded along agreeably, apparently interested in what I had to say.

I didn't know it at the time, but Mr Shí was the most important man in the room. I would later discover that he was a man of great influence (as well as razor-sharp intelligence), being the incumbent Director of Civil Affairs in Shanghai, an office that made him responsible for everything from the retired army all the way to the bin men. He was to become easily the most significant ally I made during those early years in China, and, later, a dear friend, of which more in a following chapter. But just then, he was simply another man in a suit.

A little later in the proceedings, our friend John, the gentleman who had invited us, came up to me and, rather discreetly, said that we had been invited to a further dinner banquet that evening and would we like to attend?

'We'd be delighted,' I beamed, 'wouldn't we, James?'

Poor James hardly had a choice.

So back we went for dinner, this time in a more intimate setting. We couldn't help notice that, although many of the same Chinese faces were there, none of the other westerners was. Only us. The food was even tastier and the spread even more lavish. But, as yet, no interests were declared on their part. All we really did was enjoy their hospitality and pass a pleasant evening getting to know our hosts. I later understood that this was *guangxi* in action. The word translates as 'relations' or 'connections', but wrapped up in its meaning is everything you need to know about how the Chinese go about their business. Politics, business, family life – it's all founded on the concept of *guangxi*. So although on the face of it we were merely passing an enjoyable evening, I believe, in fact, that God was in those meetings laying the foundation of a project that would change the way the Chinese care for their orphans for ever.

After we said our goodbyes, we were driven back to the Magnolia Hotel, where we found a Chinese wedding in full swing. I forget exactly how, but we were dragged into the celebrations. It was extraordinary, completely over the top in many ways, with the bride making several grand entrances, each time in a different coloured dress. The *baijiu* (pronounced 'bye-joe') – an evil-tasting clear liqueur that the Chinese love to drink – was flowing in abundance. Thus, by the time James and I extricated ourselves and went back to our room, we were pretty done in after the long day.

We lay back on our beds to unwind. James picked up his book. I flicked on the TV and found a football match in progress.

'Is that you shaking my bed?' James said suddenly, looking up from his book.

'What are you talking about? I'm watching the football,' I replied.

We both swung our legs onto the floor. There was a kind of rumble coming up through the bed legs. The curtains were shaking. We scratched our heads for a few moments, then I went to the window. Outside, far below, I could see people running around. That didn't seem normal. Something was going on. Then we heard people running down our corridor.

'There's that lady with the register at the end of hall,' I remembered. 'I'll go and ask her what's going on.'

As soon as I stepped out onto the landing, I saw that the door to every single room had been flung open, as if all the guests had left in a hurry. There was no sign of the little register lady at the desk down the hall. There was another rumble. It was only when I turned back to the room that these words suddenly rang in my head: 'Within this year, you are going to be in an earthquake. Wherever this happens is where God wants you to be.'

I felt pins and needles prickle up and down my spine. I wanted to pinch myself. *Was this really happening?* I could hardly believe it.

The following day, on the radio we heard that the earthquake had registered 6.4 on the Richter scale. The epicentre was some distance out in the Japanese Sea, but boy, had Shanghai felt its tremors.

'Well, my lad,' I thought to myself, 'Shanghai it is, then.'

7: Doors Opening

Do not despise these small beginnings,
for the LORD rejoices to see the work begin
(Zechariah 4:10, NLT)

The trip didn't end with Shanghai. We still had two cities left on our itinerary: Xi'an and Beijing.

There are two reasons you might have heard of Xi'an. The first is that it stands at one end of the historic Silk Road. This was the extensive network of trade routes that once linked ancient Rome in the West with the lucrative and exotic markets of Central Asia and, finally, ancient China, of which Xi'an (or Chang'an as it was known for much of its history) was the capital for many imperial dynasties. The second reason you might have heard of the place is because it is the site of the Terracotta Army.

This was the great highlight for James. He had read a lot about how the Terracotta Army was part of the magnificent necropolis (or City of the Dead) which Qin Shi Huang, the first emperor of China, had built in honour of himself more than two thousand years ago. Fascinating as the archaeology undoubtedly was, James's spat with one of the military guards on site about illegally filming on his minicam nearly got us into very hot water indeed. A story for another day, perhaps.

Our contact in the city, meanwhile, was a lady called Elizabeth, or Lizzie, Middleton, with whom Ross Patterson had put us in touch. She was another of the many committed souls we met on our journey, and was working for the local municipal orphanage in Xi'an.

When we arrived at the orphanage to meet her, Lizzie explained that her work was in something of a crisis. Earlier that year, a documentary film, made by undercover investigative journalists, had come out in the West about how China was managing (or rather mismanaging) its orphanages. Its findings were so explosive and condemning that it had spread like wildfire around the globe, much to the detriment of China's public image. For the Chinese, this was a disastrous loss of face on the global stage and, at the time, the impact of its widespread distribution was still very much a live issue.

One of China's responses to such negative press in the West had been to put a freeze on all foreign adoption programmes – and this included the programme with which Lizzie was involved.

Thus, when we arrived, she had almost twenty children staying in her small flat. These were children who had been selected for adoption by families in the West and had therefore been discharged from the state orphanage, but they were now not allowed to leave the country. This effectively left them in bureaucratic limbo, and Lizzie had stepped in to look after them so that they at least had somewhere to stay. But when we visited her, there was no immediate prospect of the Chinese authorities changing their policy, such was their fury at the loss of face from what they regarded as a slanderous investigative documentary.

Lizzie was clearly distressed at the situation and confused about how it would all turn out. We sympathised, of course, and prayed with her, but didn't know what else we could do. We bid her farewell, feeling pretty impotent to help her.

From Xi'an we flew on to Beijing, our last port of call before flying home. When we had been planning our itinerary, we had – quite speculatively – contacted the China Centre of Adoption Affairs to ask if we could come to see them. To our surprise, they had written back and said yes, they were willing to meet with us. But who the functionary would be for the meeting, we had no idea. We certainly expected nothing important to come of it.

So, bearing our letter of introduction from an officer of the Centre of Adoption Affairs, we turned up at one of those rather faceless old government buildings that are scattered about the capital, this one housing the Civil Affairs Bureau, and within that the smaller Centre of Adoption Affairs. We were then led into a meeting room, where we were greeted by some nondescript Chinese official. We sat with him for maybe an hour, talking in general terms about our interest in the welfare of children, and orphans in particular. The official was friendly and courteous, and at the end of our allotted slot he shook our hands and showed us out.

Outside, James turned to me, grinning. 'Did you see his papers?'

'What papers?' I asked, bemused.

'The ones on the desk in front of him. I read them upside down. He had a file marked "British Government" on the front, and from what I could see the rest of them were all about those blocked adoptions in Xi'an.'

'Really? So he thought we were diplomats or something?'

'I don't know. Looks like it,' chuckled James. 'Let's hope we didn't do Her Majesty any discredit!'

We certainly hadn't mentioned the blocked adoptions once.

There was only one thing left to do to complete our trip. We couldn't leave without visiting the Great Wall of China, after all!

Twenty-four hours later I was sitting at my kitchen table in Guernsey, telling Liz all that had happened. But even that close to the events, it all seemed like a dream.

However, when the phone rang a few days later, the dream proved real enough. It was the Foreign Office. They wanted to see me.

'Where?' mouthed Liz, catching the threads of my half of the conversation.

I covered the receiver. 'In London,' I hissed. 'Whitehall.'

She nodded, evidently impressed. 'What for?'

'Search me,' I shrugged.

Packing a small bag for the short trip the following Tuesday, part of me felt like a guilty schoolboy, and I scoured my mind for anything we might have done wrong. But after everything that had happened, I also felt a growing certainty that helping orphans in China was the call that God had put on my life. Perhaps this would be the next stepping stone he placed on my path.

On arrival in Whitehall, I was met by a diplomatic official. The first thing he did was to give me a tour of the Foreign and Commonwealth Office (FCO) in all its grandeur. He was perfectly friendly and obliging, so I quickly figured they hadn't whisked me to London for a dressing-down. At length, he ushered me into a rather grand meeting room, where, seated around a long corporate table, were several faces that I recognised from the big lunch meeting in Shanghai where I had met Mr Shí.

I was introduced to the general company, and the first one to address me directly was a man called Mike Wood, who represented the Overseas Development Agency (ODA), later to become the Department of Foreign and International Development (DFID).

'So come on, Robert,' he smiled, 'tell us how you did it.'

'How I did what?' I asked. I had no idea what he was referring to.

Mike gave an amused snort. 'How did you get the Chinese government to agree to it?'

'What do you mean?' I said, still none the wiser. 'Agree to what?'

'They released those orphans in Xi'an. They're now able to leave the country.'

'What?' I could hardly believe it.

'I don't know what you said to them in Beijing,' smiled Mike, 'but it seemed to do the trick.'

'There have been some communications between the Chinese and our side since the Shanghai meeting,' interrupted another diplomat, a little brusquely. 'Your name has been mentioned. It seems the civil authorities in Shanghai are rather keen to involve you in any projects going forward.'

Well, this was news to me. And, frankly, I was struck dumb.

'Do you even know what was going on at that lunch meeting?' pressed the FCO man, seeing my blank face.

'Cultural exchange, wasn't it?' I grinned. That was a phrase the Chinese often liked to use.

'Not exactly.' The FCO man then began to fill me in. It seemed there was something of a backstory to the scene into which James and I had stumbled in Shanghai. He explained that this investigative documentary – which was still a live issue at this point – had put the Chinese hackles up. In fact, they had taken the loss of face on the international stage so badly that it had caused something of a diplomatic incident (hence the orphans held in limbo). Subsequently, the FCO had sent over some officials, together with representatives from two other big international NGOs, as a kind of olive branch to find a more amicable way through the mess left by the documentary makers. However, as I have already described, that meeting in Shanghai hadn't exactly gone to plan, at least from the FCO's point of view.

'What we want to know is why they invited you to that dinner and no one else. How did you arrange it?'

Well, still spiritually hot, as it were, off the back of my China trip, my first instinct was to answer, 'It's simple, really: God arranged it.' But though I believe that to be true, I realised that answer probably wouldn't wash with these Whitehall civil servants. With no more plausible explanation to offer, I wasn't sure what to say. Fortunately, I was saved by someone else jumping in with another question.

It was only much later that I came to understand the nature of the Shanghai civil authorities' interest in me. Mr Shí, who you'll remember was the Director of Civil Affairs for Shanghai, was, as I've said, a very smart man, and I believe he had two distinct motives. One was essentially practical. During our conversation in Shanghai, when I had described the concept of placing orphans within new families, he at once grasped that one of the first questions to address was how to go about finding couples willing to take responsibility for a child who is not their own. He had mentioned that, in his guise as Director of Civil Affairs, he was presently having to deal with the closure of a huge factory plant on the outskirts of Shanghai. This meant laying off thousands and thousands of its mostly female workers. His mind was always working, you see – looking for connections – and he figured that maybe these women, finding themselves without work, could be encouraged to occupy themselves with raising orphans instead. It would diminish the impact of the lay-offs and ease the pressure on his overstretched orphanages, and such a worthy cause appealed to his sense of civic duty. Two birds with one stone, as it were, which wouldn't do the price of his own political stock any harm, either.

So I think he was interested in the idea from the outset. But the second motive for wanting to involve me was perhaps even more compelling for him. If he could place a westerner within the Chinese system, but one free of the organisational group-think of the more established international NGOs, then it could go a long way to drawing the sting out of the bad diplomatic blood that had arisen over the negative publicity his Shanghai orphanage had recently suffered. In the future, if western humanitarians ever came knocking on his door demanding a look-see, he could point to me, a westerner already embedded within the country's own child welfare structure: *We already have someone with visibility into everything that we are doing,* could be the line.

In a sense, I was the perfect man for him. I had experience in the field; I had a very clear vision for how the current situation could be improved; I came without any agenda being pushed into China by a foreign government or by an international NGO. Better yet, if the system was essentially still run by the local Chinese authorities in Shanghai, then who would get the credit if a new programme of family placement actually worked?

As I said, Mr Shí was a shrewd man.

But I couldn't see all this yet, so I had little to tell these Whitehall officials.

Still, to their credit, they saw in me an opportunity and not an obstacle. In particular, Mike Wood, the ODA man, appeared to believe in my vision to help orphaned and abandoned children have opportunities for family life. He said if I was willing to progress the Shanghai connections and see where they might lead, then he would support me, and I should apply for ODA funding.

But even with support inside the British government, the situation was delicate, and the FCO advised me not to make any involvement too public. There was clearly a willingness in both China and the UK to make something happen, but the plan needed to be kept under wraps for the time being. I foresaw that this could cause problems with my employers back in Guernsey, since they couldn't hope to understand my mysterious new connections with China if they were kept in the dark.

As I flew home, there was a lot turning over in my mind as I gazed down at the grey rollers of the English Channel passing below. Before I had gone to China, I couldn't see the shape of my involvement there – that was if I could be of any use at all. I suppose I had imagined I might go and find out a bit about how they were caring for orphans around China, maybe write a report or two with a few recommendations that might have some influence on those in charge. But what Mike Wood and his colleagues were suggesting seemed to be an altogether bigger project. As the drone of the engines dropped in pitch in preparation for our approach into Guernsey Airport, it occurred to me for the first time that I might have to move my whole family out to China.

Was I ready for that?

Were they?

8: Stepping Stones

Your word is a lamp for my feet,
a light on my path.
(Psalm 119:105)

In the period that followed, I felt a bit like a puppet in the hands of the Grand Designer – or at least a character in his story – as he led me from person to person, from connection to connection, each of which would prove to be an important cog in the machine he was constructing to bring great change to China. God was building a team: the right people at the right time.

Even so, his plan didn't unfold without complications.

Contact with the Foreign Office continued after I arrived home in Guernsey, and once they had decided to accept my involvement, they swung in behind me with great energy, becoming a reliable source of support ever after. The ODA's, then the DFID's, support proved a little more complicated over time, although Mike Wood was personally always behind the project; indeed, he was my biggest advocate inside the British government.

As conversations flew back and forth to China, my Foreign Office contacts encouraged me to return to Shanghai to meet with Mr Shí and his subordinates, including a man called Mr Li, a civil servant attached to Mr Shí's office, and a Dr Zhou, who was responsible for running the orphanage in Shanghai, the official title of which was the Shanghai Social Welfare Institution. 'Don't tell your employers what it's about,' the FCO mandarins counselled. 'Take leave when you go out there.'

Well, that was easier said than done, and although my employers at the Children's Board were perfectly happy with my work for them, they surely started to wonder what I was up to. Moreover,

I wasn't in a position to fly myself out to China at the drop of a hat. With six children and a social worker's salary we had enough to get by, but we definitely were not rich. I needed funding from the UK end if I were to keep the iron hot with Shanghai.

Besides those limitations, there was something of a pull factor from another quarter in Guernsey. Our pastor, Jonathan Le Tocq, was trying to obtain on my behalf what was called a 'long licence' to stay in employment on the island of Guernsey. This was a kind of resident work permit that went beyond the standard eight years that most outsiders were granted to live and work on Guernsey. I was getting through my eight years with the Children's Board, but Jon was determined that we should stay on the island. He wanted me to come on the team to work for the church, running its youth programme. At this stage, nothing was confirmed in relation to China; it was all still fairly speculative. And while I felt in my heart that China was the road my life would be taking, I didn't have anything solid yet with which to dampen Jon's alternate plans.

Nevertheless, over the following weeks and months during 1997, a plan began to formulate between the various stakeholders. Liz and I continued to pray that God would use us in China, and while the spiritual and emotional preparation continued, no immediate door flew open.

However, during the course of 1997, two significant connections were made. The first was, in some ways, the more improbable.

One of the Foreign Office contacts with whom I was in regular communication by now was a man called Paul Davies, the Deputy Consul General in Shanghai. It was sometime during early spring that year when Paul contacted me to tell me he was coming to London and had set up a meeting with an English entrepreneur. 'You need to be there,' he said.

I hesitated. 'I don't know. I'm not sure work will wear me disappearing off to London again so soon. And the flights aren't cheap.'

'It's Richard Branson,' he replied.

'Oh.' I thought about it for a few moments. 'In that case, let me make a phone call.'

Of course, I'd heard of him. Most people in the UK have heard of Sir Richard Branson in one way or another; he's one of the highest-profile businessmen in the world. And while I had no doubt he had plenty of money, I wondered what interest he could possibly have in me.

I called James. 'Fancy meeting Richard Branson in London?' I asked, dangling the bait.

'Would I? You bet!'

'That's good. Will you pay for the flights?'

Generous as ever, James didn't bat an eyelid, and the following Tuesday we found ourselves in a black cab driving down the leafy avenues of west London on a bright spring morning, heading for Branson's London office. I say 'office' – his headquarters are managed from a very large, very beautiful town house overlooking Holland Park.

We sat waiting for him in a grand sitting room with impossibly high ceilings, gazing up at a huge replica of a Virgin Atlantic 747 suspended in the space above us. Paul thought Branson would be interested in our project because it might chime with Virgin Atlantic's bid for the London–Shanghai air route, which was coming up for tender for the first time the following year. Virgin, of course, already had its transatlantic routes in place, and it also offered flights to Hong Kong. But the contest was likely to be between Virgin and BA for the all-new Shanghai contract from the UK Civil Aviation Authority. Being able to point to a charitable project helping orphans in China, Paul explained, would surely be no bad thing for Virgin's bid.

After a few minutes, the familiar figure of Richard Branson came bounding down the stairs wearing a baggy sweater and with a bandage on his little finger. 'No handshakes today, I'm afraid,' he apologised, waggling his finger by way of explanation. 'Just broke it windsurfing on Necker.' That was the island he owned in the Caribbean. 'Surprisingly painful.'

After the introductions, he settled back into his big chair and flopped a leg over one arm. 'So,' he said, with that disarming grin of his, 'tell me about China.'

I launched into an explanation of our vision to help the orphans of Shanghai, about the problems of institutional care and the crowded conditions in the orphanages in China and their under-resourced staff, and how the one-child policy was fuelling the whole problem. But as I continued speaking, it was soon obvious that his attention was waning. He was only half-listening, shifting around in his seat, tuning in and out of the conversation to deal with other things. Before I'd finished, I already sensed this wasn't going to work.

As he got up to leave, I felt deflated and disappointed. The whole thing had been a complete waste of everyone's time. We gathered up our things to go and he was halfway up the staircase when he suddenly stopped and turned around.

'Roger!' he cried. (He always called me Roger, I don't know why.) 'Let's do it! You go to Shanghai, and I'll support you.'

As the three of us descended the stone steps outside his office, Paul could barely contain his excitement. 'That's just amazing! Amazing!' he said.

'No, it's not,' replied James, ever with his deadpan timing. 'It's just God providing Rob with his transport manager.'

It would be a while before Virgin would be able to offer that kind of direct logistical support to Shanghai, although its London–Hong Kong route was indeed a great blessing. Virgin *did* eventually win the contract from the UK Civil Aviation Authority some time later, in December 1999, and the London–Shanghai route was to prove a Godsend for Virgin Atlantic (as well as for us). It was more or less its new Shanghai route alone that kept Virgin from going out of business post-9/11, when its transatlantic revenue all but dried up.

In the meantime, I had identified another supporter closer to home on the island of Guernsey. While I had been keeping the China plans fairly close to my chest, I did share the vision with a select few, if I thought it expedient to do so. One of these was a very warm-hearted lady whom I shall call Mrs Forester. Mrs Forester was a Christian. She also happened to have a big heart for China, and besides this, she was a multimillionaire.

Excited by what we could do out there together, our friendship grew through the course of 1997. Towards the end of the year, it was clear from my ongoing discussions with Shanghai that the time had come for me to visit our contacts there again in person, and Mrs Forester very kindly offered to fund the trip.

She had a number two – a kind of financial manager – with whom I dealt regarding all the more prosaic day-to-day matters. As we put together a plan for my second trip to China in December 1997, he wanted to arrange a meeting, involving the three of us, out in Hong Kong. I, meanwhile, had been coming to the conclusion that Mrs Forester, although personally supportive of me, had a rather different vision from me for how we should help orphans in China, and this difference would eventually cause our roads to part. Her preference was to use her financial means to build a beautiful new orphanage in Hong Kong and to care for children coming out of mainland China there by providing them with the best resources available.

My vision was altogether more strategic. I wanted to see a complete overhaul of the system of orphan care across the whole of China. Merely creating another orphanage in Hong Kong and organising nice tea parties for the children held no interest for me.

Notwithstanding these differences, we still planned to meet in Hong Kong to discuss the orphanage proposal before I went on to Shanghai. Her number two even suggested that we ask Virgin to fly them out to Hong Kong business class and free of charge, since Branson was now supposed to be backing me. But I told him that was a bad idea. I didn't want to take advantage of Branson's goodwill; our relationship was still in its fledgling stage.

In the event, they didn't turn up to the meeting in Hong Kong, although they did generously pay for all of my flights on that second trip. I didn't know it at the time, but that relationship was about to go sour. Very sour, indeed.

Back in Shanghai, I greeted my government contacts there like old friends. I was travelling alone this time, although David Gotts – the young man we had meet in the Changsha orphanage from the previous trip – had flown in to be present at our meetings as well.

Mr Shí was still the driving force (and senior authority) behind what we intended to do, but when it came to the detail, he had delegated the project to his number two, Mr Li, and the section chief of Shanghai Civil Affairs, a Mrs Gao.

The main purpose of this trip was to formalise my involvement with the Shanghai government. Throughout the year, there had been discussions about bringing me in as a social care consultant, perhaps flying me back and forth from the UK as and when I was needed. Eventually, however, all parties concluded that the position should be something altogether more permanent, and more present.

Thus there was to be an official contract-signing ceremony. I was being appointed as Senior Consultant in Social Welfare on an initial three-year contract. The irony was not lost on my Chinese friends that they were appointing a father of six children to assist a country overcome by the unintended consequences of its one-child policy. At that time, given that the concept of family placement in China was entirely new, they had no word or expression for it in Mandarin. So, they had to make one up. They had settled on *jiatíng jiyàng* (to use its Pinyin form). This translates as 'family welfare', and that is what went in my contract.

The meeting was rather formal this time, and was held in a big conference room in the Civil Affairs Bureau building. There were a number of officials present, all seated around the large, red-leather table. Mr Li was chairing the meeting.

'We need a name for the contract,' he said, in his rather direct manner.

'Well, you know my name,' I returned. 'Use that.'

'No,' he smiled. 'If you come and work for us, you need a *Chinese* name.' He went on to explain that, since I was to become part of Chinese officialdom, all documents and letters approved or originating from me would need to be stamped with my official seal, which had to contain only Chinese characters. 'Your name is very important.'

What I didn't realise was just how important their choice was going to be. If I wanted a seal on all that God had led me to, this was to be it.

For about twenty minutes, Mr Li and his colleagues had an animated conversation, which I gathered was all about what would be the most suitable name for me. Every now and then they would look across the room at me, scratch their chins a bit, then dive back into the debate. Eventually they all leaned back in the boardroom chairs with smiles on their faces, satisfied that they had come up with the winning combination of characters that encapsulated me best.

One of the officials got to his feet. 'I am pleased to say we have found your name. But first we want to tell you what your name means, since the meaning of a person's name is very important in our culture. Yours means this: 'As many stars as there are in the sky, you will be father to children in China.' Your name shall be *Lao Bà-Bà*. Something like Old Father.'

My heart started racing. What had he just said? Those were exactly the same words that David Devenish had spoken over me four years earlier in Guernsey. Back then I had had no idea of their significance. At the time I had guessed that they might signify something to do with the youth ministry on the island, if they meant anything at all. But God had meant something so much greater.

I suddenly found myself thinking of an encounter between God and Abraham in the book of Genesis, which I had read about in my Bible many times. Abraham is old and childless when God tells him to step outside. 'Look up at the sky,' God tells Abraham, 'and count the stars – if indeed you can count them . . . So shall your offspring be' (Genesis 15:5).

I had held on to David Devenish's word, not knowing when or how it might be fulfilled, but believing God and trusting that his understanding was far greater than my own. And now here were some Chinese officials – none of whom, as far as I knew, were Christians – who, after a long debate, had come up with the exact wording of the same promise that God had made to me through his servant David Devenish.

Now, at last, I felt God's seal on me – that he was bringing all the pieces together, confirming the plans we had to go to China and place orphans within families. How many orphans were there in China at the time? I had no idea – but I was fairly sure the number was more than I could count.

As many stars as there are in the sky . . .

With the ink of my signature barely dry on my new contract, I found myself on the plane home. As I watched the bright lights of Shanghai fall away through the little window, it occurred to me that my Chinese name was actually a back-to-front version of the word David had given me. He had said I would be 'father to as many children as there are stars in the sky'. Mulling this over, I picked up an in-flight magazine and flicked through its pages. Every article was written in English and in Mandarin. I suddenly noticed that Chinese script reads from right to left. So, in fact, the meaning of my name was exactly as David Devenish had said it.

I marvelled at how God knows us in every way, that he is sovereign over our lives and able to confirm to each one of us the plans and purposes he has for us, exactly as and when we need it.

I settled back into my seat for the long flight home, basking in the thought of what a good Father we have in him.

As I mentioned before, during this period God had started to connect me with some remarkable people. One was a man called de Vic Carey, a High Court judge whom I had got to know well during my time working for the adolescents' secure unit. De Vic linked me with a man named John Langlois (pronounced 'longlay'), who would prove to be an inimitable support not only to the organisation, but also to me personally. He was a lawyer and a prominent politician on the island, and also, I discovered, a Christian. The first time I met with him, he invited me to share my vision with him, and he listened carefully as I recounted the story of all that had happened in China, the doors that God had already opened for me and the systemic change I hoped to bring there.

When I had finished, he looked me straight in the eye. 'I believe this is of God,' he said. 'I'm going to give this priority over everything else.' He wasn't exaggerating. Over the years, he has proved himself to be as formidable a mentor and ally to me as anyone I know.

Through Mike Woods at DFID, I was being encouraged to apply for funding from the British government for the project. For this to happen, I needed to set up a charitable vehicle that could receive the money. Thus, the idea of Care for Children was born, in a sense out of necessity.

I began to draw together a small group of trusted individuals to make this happen. My friend James was an obvious choice, as was John Langlois, with his legal expertise and political nous. The fourth person I wanted to involve was a guy named Bill Cody. Bill and his wife, Jill, had been missionaries in Thailand, and they had also worked with Jackie Pullinger in Hong Kong. Liz and I had met them through the New Frontiers network some years before and we had since become good friends.

The four of us held our first meeting in a little pub in the village of Olney in Buckinghamshire shortly after Christmas and my return from Shanghai. As soon as it came to the question of the DFID funding, we all agreed we needed to move forward and set up Care for Children as it required. (We four would be the original board members.) I explained to them that DFID was ready and willing with the money, according to Mike Woods, but I would still have to apply for the grant according to the proper procedure, which would involve submitting a long and detailed application.

'The problem is,' I told them, 'I'm still working flat out for the Children's Board. There's no way I can spare the time it would take to do this thing justice.' And clearly, no one else had the expertise to be able to write the application in my stead.

We could all see the problem, but as yet no solution. We closed the meeting in prayer, each speaking in turn. When it came to James, he said, 'Lord, please make a way for Rob to be able to write this application.'

There's a book called *God Knows You're Human* by Terry Virgo, the man who led the Stoneleigh Bible Week for all those years. In it, he writes, 'Before God can use strong people he has to weaken and humble them. The truth is that God has to deal with the mighty so that they become aware of their weakness; then he can fill them with his power and use them.'*

Let's be honest. How many of us have ever asked God to weaken and humble us?

But that's what he was about to do to me.

---

* Terry Virgo, *God Knows You're Human* (New Wine Press, 2009.)

9: Accused

You intended to harm me, but God intended it for good to
accomplish what is now being done, the saving of many lives.
(Genesis 50:20)

I got into work the following Monday to discover some ugly news
waiting for me.

My boss at the Children's Board, a man named Steve Le Tissier,
who had for a long time been a personal friend, called me into
his office.

'Robert,' he began, his voice rather stiff, 'there has been an
allegation against you.'

'An allegation?' I stammered. 'What on earth for?'

'I'm afraid I can't share the details as yet . . .'

'But that's crazy.'

'I'm sorry,' he said more firmly, fixing me in the eye. 'I'm
suspending you from work on full pay while we investigate.'

I felt a horrible, hollow feeling open like a crack of doom inside
my chest. I continued to press him for the identity of my accuser
and for the details of what it was I was supposed to have done.
But Steve insisted he could not tell me anything.

This was devastating. Steve and I were squash partners, for
heaven's sake, but now it seemed he was prepared to believe
someone else's word over mine. I couldn't begin to imagine what
it was about, but from his tone it was clearly serious.

I drove away from the office to go and meet Liz, who had just
dropped the girls off at school. As I told her the news, the shock
of it suddenly brought tears to my eyes. I knew how accusations
in my industry could stick. I was overwhelmed with a feeling of
rejection and despair, but most of all I was boiling inside with

the injustice of it – to be suspended from work without any kind of explanation. Would this mean I would lose my job? What if this affected what was building in China? My reputation was on the line – and if that was shot down, what future did I have? I racked my brain to think who could have made a complaint against me, but I had no idea.

For the two weeks of my suspension, not one friend phoned me. Rumours were flying around the island – and mud always sticks more easily when the aspersions cast are about childcare. I felt completely isolated and alone. John Langlois was away at the time in the US. Eventually I managed to track him down and get him on the phone. I must have sounded quite desperate because he told me to calm down.

'You mustn't fight this,' he said. 'Do nothing. Let God deal with it . . . "Vengeance is mine, says the Lord," eh?'

'Yes, but–'

'I know it's an incredibly bitter pill to swallow. But you have no choice. You don't know your accuser, you don't know the accusations, so how can you possibly know how to respond?'

I stood silent on the other end of the receiver.

'All you can do is sit tight and put yourself in God's hands.'

I knew he was right.

I put down the phone feeling as bleak as I ever had. I jumped in the family car and drove out to the southern cliffs where Liz and I had walked on our first trip to the island. The dark cliffs and swirling seas seemed hostile now and full of foreboding. I screamed my frustration into the January winds blasting off the ocean, calling on God to vindicate me. But vindicate me against what, I didn't know.

I didn't understand why he would let this happen. Here I was, trying to obey him, offering myself to go to the ends of the earth to serve orphans, just as he had called me to do. Why, now, was my whole career suddenly in jeopardy? Didn't he care?

My screaming faded away to silence. And even though I felt completely broken by this, I also began to feel closer to God than ever before. In my isolation, I had little to go on but the written word. My daily Bible reading took on new life, seeming to speak directly into what I was feeling each day. I drew strength and encouragement from that.

I read about Joseph in the book of Genesis, he of the techni-coloured dreamcoat fame. God spoke to Joseph in powerful and vivid dreams about his plans for Joseph's future, and after my 'naming' in China I could relate to that: that feeling of being somehow special, chosen by God for something specific. But soon after God gave those dreams to Joseph, things went south pretty far and pretty fast. Betrayed by his brothers, sold into slavery, falsely accused and sitting in prison in a foreign land, it would have been very easy for Joseph to give up on God. But he didn't. And now, falsely accused myself, I wasn't about to either.

I found that those solitary walks along the clifftops became times of solace and revelation. I would watch the awesome power of the ocean smashing against those rocks, and it made me think of the far more awesome power of the Creator who made all things, who made the winds and the seas and the mountains. And I realised this was crunch time for me. Would I snivel and whine and quake in fear? Or would I praise God in the midst of my strife, and trust in him, despite my situation?

I didn't want to be lukewarm any more. I refused to be a 25-per-cent follower of Christ, or even a 75-per-cent one. It was all or nothing. 'Everything I have belongs to you,' I bellowed into the wind, knowing that God would hear me. I sucked down a few breaths of cold air, and then dropped my voice to a murmur. 'I don't want to hold on to my life so tightly . . . Even if I'm stripped of my job, my reputation, my calling . . . I trust you . . . I trust you, Lord.'

At the end of those two weeks, Steve finally revealed to me my accuser. As you've probably guessed, it was Mrs Forester, the wealthy lady who had funded my recent trip to China, who had made the formal accusation. Earlier, I described how our visions for how we should help the orphans of China had diverged quite markedly. But I had never suspected that this would lead to such bad blood between us.

With hindsight, I now know that the accusations had their origins not with Mrs Forester herself, but with her number two, a man who was an acerbic character, to say the least, and who had been briefing her against me. Steve reported that he had called into question my social work qualifications – did I even have any? What was I really up to every time I went off to London with so little explanation? And, worst of all, I was accused of misusing funds on behalf of our nascent charity, Care for Children, of which, at that stage, Mrs Forester was a supporter. To this day, I don't really know why her assistant had taken against me. But at least this was all now in the open.

The most serious of these charges was undoubtedly that of misusing her funds. But by the time I was filled in on the situation, my friend John Langlois had already reimbursed her every penny from the China trip, so at least she had no hold over me in that regard. Even so, the suggestion of dishonesty still lingered.

'Do you believe her?' I asked Steve, my boss.

'I'm sorry, Robert. She's an upstanding member of the community. I have to look into it,' he replied, this time unable to look me in the eye. I suspected there was some pressure from other quarters. The political overseers of the Children's Board were a small group of politicians whom everyone on the island dreaded – incredibly severe and sticklers for process. They wouldn't let slip any allegation of corruption or backhanders. It didn't matter that I had served the Children's Board well for nearly six years.

It took another month for the investigation to reach its conclusion. In the end, I was completely exonerated from all the charges – and personally vindicated, as I had prayed. All the allegations were found to be false and without basis.

John Langlois, who as well as being a lawyer was one of the senior members of the Island Parliament, was with me at the hearing. He stood up and challenged Steve Le Tissier, as Director of the Children's Board. 'What are you going to do for Robert now?' he demanded.

'There's no question,' was Steve's answer. 'We will welcome him back to his position at the Children's Board on full pay.'

'No, no,' said John, a mischievous twinkle in his eye. 'Robert won't be coming back. He needs three months of full pay as compensation.'

Somewhat grudgingly, Steve agreed to these terms. Within a month of the Olney meeting I had left my employment and I now had three months to plan our move to China, as well as to charge my way through the DFID funding application, which I now had sufficient time to complete – with a little help from John and a sister organisation called Tearfund.

There was no doubt: God had answered James's prayer in Olney, but not in the way I, or anyone else, could have guessed. I can't say it was a comfortable ride, but then God calls us out to adventure. If comfort was all he wanted for us, he would leave us sitting right at home.

In the book of Genesis, Joseph experienced a miraculous restoration and later a wonderful reconciliation with his family. Some years after, when their father Jacob had died, his brothers were fearful that Joseph might finally exact his revenge. But his answer to their fear was this: 'You intended to harm me, but God intended it for good to accomplish what is now being done, the saving of many lives' (Genesis 50:20).

Our time in Guernsey was nearing its end. The time for God's plan to be put into action was fast approaching. With this ordeal behind us and the prospect of China ever more real, this was no longer only about me. It was about all of us: me, Liz and our six children.

Since her experience at Stoneleigh the previous summer when she had realised for the first time that my burden for China might soon become her burden as well, Liz had resolved simply to be obedient to God. 'If you want me to go, I'll go,' she had prayed, and that was her attitude. She didn't particularly like the idea and, if truth be told, she harboured a fair amount of trepidation about what life would be like for us, especially for the children. But she wanted to be faithful above all things, and when asked by friends whether she ought to go to China to take a look, she would answer that she didn't need to see it. God's call was enough for her.

Yet some of her friends started to notice that something wasn't quite right: there seemed to be a measure of denial mixed in with her staunchly obedient position. One of them said to her, 'That's all very well for you, Liz, but it would still be wise to go out there, not for your sake, but for the children's.'

She received this as sound counsel. 'It sounds like something God would say,' she conceded, and so she agreed to accompany me on my next trip out to Shanghai, in March 1998.

Liz hadn't travelled nearly as widely as I had. In fact, she had never been outside Europe. So the sights and sounds and smells of Shanghai were bound to be overwhelming for her. In 1998, Shanghai was the fastest-developing city in the world. One-fifth of the world's cranes were busy throwing up one skyscraper after another in the marshy district of Pudong, the city that would soon become Asia's answer to Manhattan.

Some of our backers had graciously put us up in a very luxurious hotel in downtown Shanghai, not far from where all this construction activity was continuing apace. The contrast between the glittering atrium and vast bedroom of our hotel against the poverty in the streets and the construction site wastelands was beyond anything Liz had ever witnessed, and I could see it was hard for her to process.

Despite the long journey, after checking in and dropping our luggage in our room, we went straight off to the orphanage. Although I had visited before and had described some of the conditions to Liz, it's very different when you see something like that with your own eyes. One nursing ward in particular made a big impression on her – the one where the infant children slept. The metal-framed cots, the pervading smell of stale urine, babies whimpering and unattended, their eyes, already dull with despair, staring up at the ceiling. Each cot had a bottle attached to the side grille, rather like in a hamster cage, with the teat protruding into the crib. The babies had to roll over and suck on the teat to feed themselves. It seemed like a place devoid of hope. Even the memory of it is disturbing.

Liz just wanted to go and pick the children up and take them in her arms, but of course she couldn't do that for all of them. She remembers being particularly struck by the sight of an *ayi*, or nurse, changing one of the babies. They didn't have anything like the nappies used in the West, only a filthy rag wrapped around their loins. Some of the older children had shaved heads and sores on their scalps. It was shocking, even for me, to see this afresh through Liz's eyes.

When we came away from the place and drove back to the hotel through that dirty, noisy city, Liz was subdued, to say the least. I decided to leave her alone to process what she had seen.

That night, still jet-lagged from the long flight, she lay in our enormous bed gazing up at the ceiling, tears welling silently in her eyes. 'I can't do it, Lord,' she murmured in the darkness. 'I just don't think I can do this.'

In the silence that answered her, she felt God say, 'You don't have to.'

In that moment, she felt completely released from the obligation she had put herself under simply to obey. However, the answer of her heart to God's word was, 'But I *want* to help those children, Lord.' She lay weeping beside me as God filled her heart with his peace, and suddenly she was sure that everything would be all right. God's hand was in this and whatever would happen to us and our children, it would be all right. Now her yes was a free choice, now it was filled with new meaning because God was giving her the chance to say no. She knew the cost now, but she was still willing to bring our children to this strange land to start a life here, all for the sake of those desperate little creatures in that orphanage.

That one, and hundreds like it, across the country.

Upon our return to the UK, things moved quickly.

While I was still working on the DFID application, the board completed the formalities of establishing Care for Children as an official charity in preparation for the receipt of any government funding. Besides this, through Richard Graham – another Foreign Office man based in Shanghai – I had been connected with two other influential figures. The first was Sir John Chalstrey, a former Lord Mayor of London who, during his tenure, had visited Shanghai and signed an official declaration of friendship between the two cities. The other was Sir David Brewer – who later also became Lord Mayor of London – an expert on China, having done business with the Chinese for decades and accompanied every British Prime Minister since Margaret Thatcher on Britain's many trade delegations there. He was head of the British–China Business Council at the time. Both men joined Care for Children's board. And as the quality and influence of our supporters grew, so, too, did my confidence.

After our last trip to Shanghai, I now had a start date: September 1998. This was less than four months away. When he heard this, John Langlois counselled me to arrange some preparation time for us as a family – preferably somewhere in Asia – before we launched into China itself. The idea was to prepare ourselves to be embedded in a new culture, and also for me to receive more focused training about living and working 'in country'. We settled on Singapore, where Ross Patterson was based.

The time had come to tell the children that we had the green light. We sat them all around the kitchen table one evening and set out the plan.

'It's really happening now,' I told them. 'We're moving to China.'

All of them said they were willing to go. Even so, Lois – our second eldest daughter who was eleven at the time – burst into floods of tears. Of course, we had expected a strong reaction because it was no small step that we were taking, but over the coming days, Lois continued to be far more upset than the others and we didn't know why. We comforted her as best we could, thinking she was distressed about leaving behind her friends, and that she would get used to the idea in time.

It was only several months later, when we were already in China, that she told us the reason she had been so upset. The year before, her class had done some sort of project at school about Christianity in China, and through this Lois had learned about the persecution of the underground church there and about how many Christians had been martyred for their faith. In her eleven-year-old mind, our decision to move to China was tantamount to declaring we were going there to die for our faith. The fact that she was still willing to go, while believing she was most likely going to her death, still swells me with pride. But that's Lois for you. She has always had the heart of a lion.

It was interesting to consider how my prayer life had developed over the years. From a bleating cry for salvation in the belly of a submarine to our family life now, when everywhere we looked there was something else to pray for: money, health, the children's safety, the meal ahead, health and sickness, funding outcomes, favour with figures of influence, travel protection, peace in uncertainty, insight for the road ahead, wisdom . . . yes, a lot of that. When you knock away the support scaffold from under your life, you soon realise how it is only through God's sustaining hand that you are even alive, let alone that you are able to achieve anything. And the time had come to take an axe to that scaffold.

In the couple of weeks before we left for Singapore, which would be the moment we left Guernsey for the last time, we put up posters and distributed flyers advertising a certain day when people could come to our house and take away more or less everything that we owned. We were cutting ties, burning bridges, casting ourselves adrift on the sea of God's providence. We gave away our car to a local friend in need. Another neighbour came and picked up our washing machine. Piece by piece our furniture disappeared from our home of six years until all we had left were the mattresses we slept on.

Each of our children were allowed to take only one suitcase with them. In addition to this, Liz sat down with each of them and put together a memory box of their most precious things from their time on the island, which we would put into storage.

I was adamant that we would leave with no ties left to the UK, which meant selling the house we still owned in Sheringham. Alas, the timing was bad. The economy had taken a nosedive, and we had to sell the house at a loss, which put us in negative equity and meant we were indebted to the bank. After praying about it, I felt I should go and see the bank manager in person and explain what we were doing.

So I soon found myself seated in front of the bank manager's desk, telling him all about Shanghai and the orphanages and what my role was to be.

At the end of it, he nodded slowly, leaned forward, apparently to check the figure on the piece of paper in front of him one last time – around twelve thousand pounds, if memory serves – then he took a big sigh, as only bank managers can, and smiled. 'I think the bank will be happy to write off the amount still owing,' he said.

Now I've seen a lot of amazing things in my life, but none of them has astounded me more than that bank manager writing off that debt. If that isn't a miracle, I don't know what is.

On the day we left Guernsey for the last time, we all gathered together in the kitchen. I looked around the table at my beautiful wife and our gang of lovely children. You could feel the excitement bubbling through each of them.

'Are you ready, then?' I smiled. I knew they had been looking forward to this last, symbolic act for some time. They gave a collective cheer and raced outside into the garden, where all our mattresses lay, awaiting their fate.

One by one we hefted each mattress over the douit – the little brook that ran through the property – and up the hillock that rose behind our house. At the top, we piled them all in a heap, and the children looked on in anticipation as I doused the pile with lighter fluid. We all stepped back as I tossed a match on after it. The flame soon caught.

And we stood there, holding hands, praying that our Father God would come with us to China, while we watched the mattresses burn.

10: School of Faith

A voice of one calling:
'In the wilderness prepare
the way for the LORD;
make straight in the desert
a highway for our God.'
(Isaiah 40:3)

Some ratter-tatter words crackled out of the tannoy over our heads. None of us understood a word. Then came the translation in heavily accented English: 'Please fasten your seatbelt in preparation for our approach into Shanghai Hongqiao International Airport.'

I looked over to Liz on the other side of the aircraft, each of us book-ending the row of six blond heads between us. It was 12 September 1998. The first day of our new life in China. Rachel was thirteen, Lois eleven, Megan nine, Anna seven, and the twins Josh and Joel were just five years old.

Our time in Singapore was fading into memory. A pleasant one, true, where I had spent the mornings training with Ross Patterson while Liz homeschooled the children. In the afternoons we would all run about outside in the monsoon rains, the children wearing nothing but their swimsuits, much to the amusement of the local Singaporeans.

After Singapore, we had ducked back to England for a brief interlude before our final departure for China. I had meanwhile managed to complete the DFID application, but we still had no decision from them as to whether Care for Children would receive the funding or not. One or two voices of counsel had suggested delaying our launch until the money came through, but I had a strong feeling that it was important to honour the date that had been agreed with Mr Shí and his colleagues.

My instinct was well founded, it turned out.

We were met at the airport by not one, but two minibuses – one from some friends connected to an American church in Shanghai, the other from the Chinese government. Not wanting to cost the Chinese any face, we piled into the one they had provided and followed the Americans' minibus to the Rainbow International Hotel, where our friends had kindly offered to put us up for one night. It was another beautiful hotel. We were staying in a gorgeous suite, big enough to accommodate all eight of us. A wonderfully soft landing into China, if you like. But we knew it couldn't last.

The next day the Chinese sent over another minibus and took us to a local hotel in another part of town. This time we were on the twenty-first floor and all eight of us had to squeeze into two moderate-sized rooms. While I went off to my first day of work at the Shanghai orphanage – officially titled the Shanghai Social Welfare Institution – Liz had to somehow make do with only a large flask of boiling water (standard to each room) and a collection of instant noodles and porridge to look after the children and somehow keep them occupied.

'There was a lot of drawing,' she reported the first night.

What the children loved best, apparently, was going up and down in the lift. When they weren't drawing and joyriding the lift, Liz attempted some fresh air – something not easy to come by in central Shanghai. The road immediately outside the hotel was four lanes wide and extremely busy. Liz didn't dare attempt to cross with only herself to monitor the six children, so they were confined to walking up and down the pavement on the hotel side of the street. As you might imagine, after five days of this, Liz was pulling her hair out.

Meanwhile, I had made a start.

The main thing I had taken away from my time in Singapore from Ross Patterson about how best to manage cross-cultural situations was this: be all eyes and ears at first. Keep my mouth shut. Watch and listen and try to understand. This was the approach I had resolved to take for at least the first six months or so. This was also what Hudson Taylor had done back in the day. (In fact, 'What would Hudson Taylor do?' was not a bad question to keep in mind.)

So when I arrived that first morning at the orphanage and was greeted by Dr Zhou, his opening suggestion that I deliver a lecture to the staff didn't exactly align with my intended approach. But, whatever my reservations, the staff were assembled, and I stood at the front and had to start talking.

Within five minutes several people started playing with their phones, or got up to go out to the toilet. After seven or eight minutes, a few newspapers had been unfurled and were being noisily leafed through. Towards the end of the talk, I noticed a small huddle at the very back of the room had a card game up and running. To say I was a little discouraged is an understatement. But what I didn't realise at the time – but soon figured out for myself – was that this was a completely normal part of Chinese culture. No one bothered to listen much when someone in authority stood up and started speaking. So I certainly didn't need to take it personally.

On only my second day in Shanghai, there was an unexpected complication when I received a phone call from an American who told me he represented a university in the US. He was furious because the Chinese government, so he said, had also offered him a contract to work in the orphanage. If we hadn't arrived on the date we had agreed, the contract would almost certainly have been given to this man. I suddenly understood why I had felt so keenly the need to get to China, in spite of several things still being unresolved. We had needed to be there on time, or else the project could have easily died in its cradle. It was clear from my conversation with the American that our approaches were at polar opposites. I had come to China with a heart for the Chinese people and a passion to serve them – to empower them and lift them up. This man, on the other hand, was scathing about the government, scathing of their systems of child welfare, and scathing of Mr Li and the Shanghai Civil Affairs department.

As soon as I put the phone down, I realised I needed to tell Mr Li about the situation. When I did, he was very grateful, and I'm sure this set the tone for open and honest communication between us. It certainly seemed to prompt him into action. The next day he came to the orphanage and we sat down and started working on the bare bones of the programme together and creating a team of people who would then put it into action. The key appointment was a lady called Lu Laoshi (which means 'Teacher Lu'). She was going to run the programme from the Chinese side, which first meant working with me to train up the staff in preparation for the first placements of children with families outside the orphanage.

By the end of the first week, I at least was feeling on a firmer footing at work. Liz, on the other hand, was at her wits' end.

'I just can't do it any more,' she said, after five days of incarceration with our tribe of blond terrors. 'We're going mad up there.'

I could see she wasn't joking. I decided to call Mr Shí, my great patron in Shanghai, and he gave me some brilliant advice.

'Get the children in a school. And then get a house next to the school. After that, it doesn't matter where you are.' He reasoned that as long as we had a school near our house, I could get into work each day without too much trouble.

Remarkably, although the late 1990s was a period when the government was cracking down on the church and Christian organisations, we found out about a Christian school, called the American Concordia International School, which had just opened in the district of Pudong, and which at the time was barely more than an area of rural marshland.

The school was located next to a little village called Jinqiao. We decided to visit, and they were delighted to see us. They only had twelve students and had been on their knees in prayer, desperate for more children to come. And then we turned up with six of them, pouring out of the minibus which Mr Shí's Civil Affairs Bureau had lent to us. After a tour of the place, which didn't take long, the school seemed fine to us. It was at least an option. The question was where we would live.

Immediately opposite the school was a new development comprising a number of very large and completely empty houses. Everything around them was bare; everything was dusty. The development was called Beverley Hills – needless to say, it was nothing like its namesake. In fact, it was a good example of cross-cultural miscommunication. Whoever had financed the development had constructed a collection of enormous houses, some of them with as many as thirty-six bedrooms, working on the assumption that international companies would behave like Chinese companies – in other words, when they sent their people overseas, their employees would all live together under one roof. The developer had apparently had no concept that western companies simply don't do that, and that each family unit would prefer to live in its own dwelling.

The whole development had stood empty for two years by the time we were being shown around a house with seven bedrooms – enough to house a child in each one. The rent was well within our budget, despite the size of the place, because there was zero demand for the houses at that time.

Liz only had one reservation. 'It's like a desert out here,' she said. And it was true. Although there was the little village on one side of the new development, all the construction activity in the area did make the landscape appear rather bleak.

'Let's go to church and see if God speaks to us,' I replied with a wink.

So, that first Sunday we went to the Hengshan Community Church in the heart of Shanghai. The service was very structured, not quite what we were used to, coming as we did from a New Frontiers church in Guernsey. But we went along with the worship and all took our seats as the English pastor climbed up into his pulpit to give his sermon.

'Listen!' he exclaimed rather dramatically, pointing a finger into the congregation, more or less where we were sat. 'God might speak to you today . . .' He then started laying out the theme of his talk. It was to be about Elijah, the Old Testament prophet. 'Elijah,' he declared, 'went and lived in the desert. You could say he was in the school of faith.'

He didn't really need to go on. Liz was already digging an elbow in my ribs. 'That's God, that is,' she mouthed at me, her eyes wide with astonishment. It certainly seemed like it. And so our school of faith in the desert was where we would begin.

We moved in the next day, the first family ever to live in the Beverley Hills development in Pudong, paying a rent of two thousand renminbi (RMB) a month (roughly equivalent to two hundred US dollars, which even then was insanely cheap).

These days the whole district looks like Singapore. It would be some of the most expensive real estate in China, possibly even the world. To give you some idea of the contrast, that tiny school of twelve is today a campus of three thousand.

'At least each child has their own room,' we thought, even if we felt ourselves somewhat out on a limb. Rachel, our eldest, even had her own flat. Behind her door was a large double bedroom, a bathroom with two sinks, a sitting room and a huge walk-in wardrobe. It felt like we had gone from the sublime to the ridiculous and back again all in the space of our first week.

Although the other houses in the development were empty, the village of Jinqiao, which our bedroom looked out over, was very much alive. Almost immediately, we started visiting and getting to know the locals.

In those days, Jinqiao was almost rural. Most of the dwellings there were of a very crude construction – often, the concrete breeze blocks from which they were built were still visible and unclad. There was a small waterway that ran through the village, usually clogged with rubbish, which had steep, dusty banks. The nearby allotment strips of Chinese spinach (*po cài*) made a fairly ripe contribution to the general air quality if the wind was blowing the wrong way; from our window we would watch the local farmers ladling human waste from the communal latrines over the rows of little green plants in the field.

It was basic. Sanitation left a lot to be desired and, of course, the villagers didn't have much at all. But there was always something going on. In the warmer months, folk would sit outside drinking beer and talking and smoking, or playing the various board games that the Chinese love, or hanging around the little street vendor stalls selling roasted sweetcorn, or 'smelly tofu' as we called it (it smelled like old socks), or skewers of spiced pork, and many, many other types of street food.

We soon realised that, for most Chinese people, food is a favourite topic of conversation. A bit like the British and the weather. It's telling that the most commonplace greeting is, *Ni chi fàn-le ma?* which means, 'Have you eaten yet?' The implication is, if you haven't, then let's go and eat something together now.

With no one else to interact with, not many days passed before Liz and the children were spending as much time in the village as they were at home. After school, our children would go and play in the communal areas with the village youngsters, kicking a football or trying out the new Chinese words they had learned that day in school. On one of her early trips to the village market, Liz noticed a withered, elderly lady sat on her doorstep, shelling beans or some other produce. She was obviously very poor, and had long, dirty nails and unkempt hair. Liz decided to befriend her. She took a bowl of warm water and soap, sat down next to her and offered to wash her hands and cut and clean her nails.

At first the old woman must have been bemused by the offer, but she, and later several others, let Liz do it, and soon they were quite charmed. It became a regular point of contact, and it wasn't long before most of the older womenfolk in the village had the most wonderfully manicured and moisturised hands you ever saw.

Of course, I spent the working day at the orphanage, but after work I, too, would go out into the village, thirsty to learn more about our neighbours, how they lived life and how they thought.

Somehow I managed to identify the elder of the village, a man named Lao Yu, who proved to be a cheery old fellow with an infectious grin that revealed he only had about half his teeth left in his head. I used to make a habit of sitting with him in the evenings – he would share a cup of sweet tea with me and some roasted sweetcorn. At first, we just sat and enjoyed each other's company, him speaking no English and me still not having much Chinese, but it didn't seem to matter. A little later, when Ross Patterson, whose Chinese was fluent, came to visit us, he sat with me and the elder, translating everything we had wanted to know about the other and what we thought of each other. It was a good moment.

There was an element of healing to all this, too. Inevitably, the village folk had felt deeply hurt, not to mention angry, at the big housing development that had been dumped on their doorstep. Presumably they'd had little say in the matter, and it was likely that some of their own dwellings would have been destroyed to make way for the big, brash – and now empty – houses that occupied the large area of land to their west. Our willingness – as white foreigners – to interact with them, and (I hope) the spirit of curiosity and humility in which we did it, would go some way to healing that wound.

A couple of months after our arrival, with Christmas approaching, I managed to convey to Lao Yu, the village elder, an invitation to join in with our Christmas celebrations. It was an open invitation and everyone in the village was welcome to come and feast with us. Once he understood, he was absolutely delighted to accept, and he insisted that, since it was *our* cultural event, we must share some of our western cuisine with them. I was only too happy to do that, so we set about making it an occasion to remember.

We called up William and Nicky Lambert, two of our western friends from the church we were attending, and invited them to come along with food they had prepared. They entered into the spirit of the thing with great energy, although the preparation didn't run entirely to plan. William was responsible for ordering a turkey, but when he went to pick the bird up from the butcher on the day, it turned out he had ordered an enormous ham instead.

'Apparently the characters for "ham" and "turkey" are very similar,' William said, by way of explanation, as he hefted a huge hunk of meat onto the countertop in our kitchen. The ham took its place among an amazing assortment of other dishes. We had shepherd's pie, chilli con carne, mince pies, sherry trifles, lasagne and plenty more. A big spread.

When our local guests arrived, we lit a number of candles, and then our six children gave a rendition of 'Silent Night' in Chinese. Then it was time for the food. The elder, Lao Yu, stepped forward as the honoured guest. He took his bowl and started to fill it: a slice of ham, a dollop of sherry trifle, some cheese, a mince pie, a scoop of shepherd's pie, a spoonful of lasagne. Then he started to mash it all up into one big ball of food, delicately plucked a lump of his crazy mélange of western cuisine between his chopsticks and shoved it into his mouth.

'Delicious,' he declared, with a broad smile. 'Delicious!'

Of course, everyone took their lead from the elder, while we didn't dare say anything – and they did exactly the same.

'Wonderful,' they all said, munching away, and it truly was.

Meanwhile, Liz was following around the youngest children with a mop, because they were peeing all over the kitchen floor. We soon learned that Chinese toddlers didn't wear nappies; they waddled around with their nether regions exposed to the elements in leggings that looked more like cowboy chaps. But apart from the odd spillage to mop up, the evening couldn't have gone better.

Six weeks later, we were invited to celebrate the Chinese New Year in Lao Yu's own home. There, we were treated to a dizzying array of dishes, which we know included donkey meat – a delicacy reserved only for very special occasions – and, we think, dog meat as well. When one of the children asked me what it was, I growled, 'Just keep quiet and eat it!' through gritted teeth, while smiling at our hosts.

11: Getting to Work

In you the fatherless find compassion.
(Hosea 14:3)

I will not leave you as orphans; I will come to you.
(John 14:18)

We didn't waste any time in getting on with work at the orphanage.

After Mrs Lu's appointment, she and I got straight to work with our team of seven teachers and medical officers, newly picked from the orphanage staff. They were to be retrained as family placement officers. This meant learning how to assess the needs of both the children and the parents in the pre-placement stage of the programme.

I was given a translator, a young Chinese lady in her twenties called Shelley, who would shadow me through the early days. After a few months, Mr Shí sent a young man called Sun Yuan Jie, or Sunny as he preferred to be known, who became a lifelong friend and is still Care for Children's Country Manager today. He had completed a masters at the London School of Economics as a prestigious Chevening scholar. He was smart as a whip, his English was excellent, and his advice was even better.

Perhaps still smarting from my disastrous opening speech to the orphanage staff, I asked Sunny about the apparent lack of interest from them about what I was doing there and what we hoped to achieve. His answer was very perceptive, and helped me make sense of my position. He said one-third of them would hate it: the old guard who didn't like the idea of any kind of foreign meddling in Chinese affairs. One-third would be completely indifferent to my presence there. He explained that, for most of the staff, a job like that becomes their life. Their work unit *is* their life. They would eat together, work together, wash together, go on holiday together. Only at the end of the day would they go to their own separate homes. So the staff community was extremely tight. My sudden appearance among them was just another part of their daily existence, albeit a slightly novel one, so they wouldn't pay me much heed. The final one-third, though, he said – which, by and large, meant the younger contingent – *would* be interested in me and what I had been brought in to do.

When he finished explaining this to me, it occurred to me that the picture he painted could have been a lot worse. Even so, my goal was to win them all round eventually, so I was going to have to be patient, and meanwhile I needed to listen and learn.

Besides a team, a translator and an assistant, I was given a tiny box of an office. In the winter it was bone-chillingly cold, and in summer, as I would soon discover, it was hot as a furnace and swarming with mosquitoes. There was also a resident rat who would pop up from somewhere down the pipes whenever I was eating, having caught a whiff of the food. The rest of the staff weren't troubled by him at all. Pretty soon I got used to him too. I ended up calling him Roland and in time accepted him as a co-resident of my new office.

The orphanage itself, then called the Shanghai Social Welfare Institution, was housed in an old wooden building dating from 1911. It had once been run by British nuns, before the Cultural Revolution cleared them out. The fabric of the main building was in dire need of repair and refurbishment. There was another big concrete wing of six floors which served as a hospital, and behind that a playground, school and living area. The orphanage was home to around seven hundred children – about 60 per cent of whom were disabled in some way – all ruled by the rather mild-mannered Dr Zhou. Soon after my arrival, however, Dr Zhou was moved into a finance role elsewhere in the Shanghai civil administration, and his more fiery successor, Mrs Wong, took over as director of the orphanage.

With every week working on the project, I was learning more and more about Chinese culture. My forays into Pu Yu Xi Lù during my lunch breaks certainly helped. This was the little street that led from the main road to the gated entrance of the orphanage, a melting pot of Shanghai street life, rich in character. Houses had been built one on top of another like a pile of cards. I always felt they might collapse overnight, but I was proudly told by one of the owners they had been there for more than a hundred years.

Every day I passed chain-smoking old men playing Chinese pool, children pushing noodle trolleys, tofu vendors wreathed in clouds of foul-smelling steam, little corner shops where customers sat outside drinking bottles of Tsingtao with the sun on their face, pomelos piled into enormous yellow pyramids, and wicker towers of steaming dumplings. It had the hustle and bustle of a Dickensian thoroughfare, and I loved it. Every day on the walk to work I would pass cats leashed up like dogs, and one old lady who used to slop a bucket of dirty laundry water out into the gutter almost at my feet. (I swear she waited to see me coming.)

It felt like full immersion, and, of course, it helped that I was surrounded by Chinese people at the orphanage and that my work brought me into such close contact with the orphans I was trying to help. Even so, Mrs Wong wouldn't let me join the other staff in the canteen at first. 'You must eat here,' she said rather sternly, pointing into my office. I decided it was best to comply, content to let her determine how quickly I should assimilate with the rest of the staff.

So I spent my lunch breaks either in my little shoebox office or else I would grab a bowl of noodles out on Pu Yu Xi Lù and sit and try out my slowly growing vocabulary on the old men chewing sunflower seeds and shooting Chinese pool.

One day, I noticed some of the older children kicking a football around in the playground at the back of the orphanage. I went out and joined them, and was delighted to discover that several of them were actually pretty good. I found this surprising, knowing that most of them had been told they were stupid and weak all their lives – and worse, that they weren't wanted and that no one cared about them. Well, I wanted to show them that I did care. I wanted to give them hope and encouragement and to build their sense of self-worth. So I kept going out at lunchtime and having a kick-around. Before long, the kick-arounds turned into coaching sessions, and soon after that I had organised them into something resembling a proper team. I decided to call them the Shanghai Canaries, after my own beloved club, Norwich City.

Before our first match, I wrote home to an old friend, Andrew Cullan, who was the sales and marketing director at Norwich, and asked if there was any chance that he could ship eleven Norwich City youth strips out to us in Shanghai. Happily, he was game, and a few weeks later the Shanghai Canaries ran out onto the turf in glorious green and yellow in the first round of the Shanghai Schools Trophy. The youngsters took to the competition like ducks to water, and I was, of course, loving putting my old coaching skills to use. When Liverpool brought a team to Shanghai in the closed season, I contacted them and they invited the orphanage team to spend a day training with them in the Shanghai stadium.

To my amazement and utter delight, we won the whole competition, beating the American School 5–3 in the final. When the cup was presented to our captain, the Mayor of Shanghai delivered a solemn address: 'You have been losers all your life, but today you are winners,' he said. A bit harsh, I thought, but I suppose it was meant in good spirit. I was learning that such directness was typical of the Chinese. They called it as they saw it.

The very next day, at lunchtime, Mrs Wong appeared in the doorway of my office, flanked by what must have been most of the orphanage staff. 'We have come to invite you to the canteen,' she said, smiling. She held out an empty noodle bowl. 'We made this for you.' On it was written my Chinese name. I took it from her, beaming with gratitude, knowing I had passed a significant milestone on the road to full acceptance.

There was further sign of this when I returned one afternoon from Pu Yu Xi Lù with a sack full of pomelo fruit for my team. (For the uninitiated, a pomelo is a citrus fruit like a large grapefruit, but much sweeter in taste.)

'How much did you pay for them?' demanded Mrs Lu when I set them down on her desk.

'Thirty yuan,' I said.

She hit the roof. 'It should have cost you three. Here, give those to me!' She snatched the bag of fruit off me and marched out to the fruit seller to demand my money back, insisting that even though I was a foreigner, I wasn't fair game. I should only pay the local price for them. I took this as another good sign. Mrs Lu and the team were beginning to treat me as one of their own.

For the first six months, aside from coaching football, my job was to recruit and assess families for the pilot project that would place the first children from the orphanage into families. Mrs Lu was convinced that our best course of action was to find affluent families, but I was adamant that she was wrong. 'What we're looking for,' I told her, 'are resilient people who are willing to work *with* us, and who have a heart for children. Whether they're rich or poor doesn't make any difference.' That was my conviction at the time, although a few years later it would be sorely tested.

The first step was to launch a media campaign, and Mr Shí arranged for the local newspapers and TV stations to come down to the orphanage to interview us about what we were looking for. The response to the campaign blew me away. We received applications from more than seven hundred families.

At once, we got to work sifting through the applicants, looking for suitable candidates based on the assessment criteria and procedures I had learned from the British Association for Adoption and Fostering. But even after all the hours required to translate that material, it was soon obvious that a lot more work was needed to make the resources culturally sensitive.

This was clear from my very first interview.

'When you bathe the children, do you leave the door open?' I asked – a standard question in the UK, designed to safeguard children against potential abuse.

It was met with shocked stares.

'Do you walk around the house naked or wearing clothes?' I continued, forging bravely on down my list of questions.

This time, the couple's expressions showed outright horror. They filed an official complaint about me with Mrs Wong. After that, we rewrote that whole section of the assessment question-naire so that 'child protection' became about 'safe caring', an expression far less offensive to Chinese ears.

In spite of this, we did make progress and started to build up a file of eligible families ready and willing to take on the first batch of orphans.

Meanwhile, my language skills were advancing in fits and starts. I was picking up words all the time out on the street, in the village or in the orphanage, and every one of them was gold; the Chinese love any kind of effort to speak their language. At the same time, I enrolled in a formal language course at the East China Normal University. But the flaw in this plan soon became apparent. My working life was so hectic at the time that it was a rare day that I actually managed to make it across town to the university for the lesson. Most of the time I was ten or fifteen minutes late.

'You must arrive at lesson on time,' my teacher would scold me. 'It is disrespectful. You will not learn. If you come late, don't come at all!'

I would kowtow miserably and then she would ask for my homework, which invariably I hadn't done.

'You must do your homework,' she cried. 'It is disrespectful. You will not learn. If you not do homework, don't come!'

More kowtowing. And then my phone would go fifteen minutes before the lesson was due to end, owing to a crisis at the orphanage that needed my input. I would mutter my apologies and start getting up from my desk.

'You must stay to end of lesson,' she shrieked, in paroxysms of indignation now. 'It is disrespectful. You will not learn. If you not stay, don't come!'

And so on.

'Give it up,' Mr Shí told me, when I asked him about it in exasperation. 'The best way to learn is to go to the wet markets at the weekends, go to the parks, go to the squares and speak to your people at work. You will soon learn.'

So that's what Liz and I did. And some of it started to stick.

By the spring of 1999, we had started to place the first children. All of them were between the ages of three and five. There were children in the orphanage up to the age of eighteen, but many of the older children were already hardened by their life in residential care, or else severely disabled beyond the ability of any willing foster parents to look after them. Thus, the older children would have to work their way through the system into adulthood and we focused on finding the most suitable families for the younger children.

Because the numbers we were dealing with in China were so great, Mr Li and Mrs Lu wanted to accelerate the programme by placing them in batches. At first this was something I resisted strongly; in the UK, the practice was to focus on one child and one family at a time. But here we didn't have the luxury to do that, and in fact it was soon apparent that there were many positive aspects to doing it their way.

In the very first batch, we moved twenty children into twenty families in the same district. The effect of this approach was that the child and the family would not be ostracised or treated as an oddity in any way. Instead the families worked together, met together and supported one another. There was a sense of collectiveness about it, which in some ways was typically Chinese. Later, when we, as Care for Children, did an evaluation of the work achieved so far, we thought that this 'batch' approach was something that could also be done in the UK. That sense of unity was an extremely effective source of support for each individual family.

It was a joy to see, at last, our dream start to become a reality. Liz and I had always looked at the children in the orphanage in a different way from how other people looked at them. We had our eyes on the poor, weak and vulnerable with an eye to act, rather than simply to observe. Children – the smallest, weakest and most vulnerable – are so often the ones who pay the greatest price for family breakdown or disruption. Our heart's desire was to reverse this process, to turn the wheel the other way.

But, deeper than this, our compassion was underpinned by the knowledge of God as a Father who passionately cares for the orphans. We knew this from our own lives. The Bible says that before we know God, we are orphans. But he has adopted us into his family. Any understanding of orphan care must begin with an understanding of the character of God. He made the family for children, and just as there is a transformation when any person is grafted back into the family of God, so too a transformation takes place when a child's life is restored to a loving family.

Many of the parent volunteers were in their forties, having had a child of their own but wanting the opportunity to raise a second child.

We saw many positive changes in the children following their moves to their new families. Several children who had been thought to have serious learning difficulties made significant progress, far beyond what any of us could have hoped. In one extraordinary case, a child thought to be physically disabled and unable to walk suddenly started walking after being taken in by a family.

As to other improvements, in a lot of ways all that was needed was pretty basic stuff. Giving a child individual time and attention brought about tremendous progress, mainly because the starting point was so low. Many of these children didn't know their colours or their numbers, let alone how to read or write. Often, at the age of three or four they were still feeding from bottles and were not yet toilet trained. So even just basic life skills transformed these little ones from neglected little creatures with hardly any sense of themselves into the beginnings of nurtured human beings.

This development cut both ways sometimes. In an institutional environment, some children had learned how to be manipulative, playing one adult off against another. In a family environment, they could no longer do this: 'no' meant 'no' when two parents were in agreement. Establishing healthy boundaries would be a huge help to these youngsters.

Another area that was very beneficial was something called life story therapy. This is when a professional would sit down with the child and their new foster parents and work through the child's life, from the official birth certificate if there was one, where they were born (if known; sometimes a mother would leave an anonymous note with details of the baby's place of origin) through to where and when they were found and how long they had been in the orphanage's care. It was important for them to know their own story, even if it was far from ideal. A greater understanding of themselves enabled them to grow.

Tang Yishu was a fairly typical example of those early placements. She was six years old and deaf, and one of the first girls we placed. Ping, a lady in her fifties, welcomed the girl into her family. Her daughter was an English teacher and knew sign language, so between them they had something substantial to offer little Tang. We witnessed her blossom under the love of her new mother and sister, and very soon she was a completely different girl.

Most of the children we were placing were girls – something like 82 per cent – because most of the children in the orphanage were girls. This was one of the unintended consequences of the one-child policy, which at that time was in force in its strictest form.

In general, healthy boys would not be abandoned in China, only disabled ones. But girls were a different matter. In China, the birth of a boy is a cause for celebration; the birth of a girl is considered a 'small happiness'. There are Chinese sayings like,

'There are thirty-six virtues, but to be without an heir is an evil which negates them all,' and, 'A daughter married is like water poured out of the door.'

There is a practical reason behind this prejudice. In China – as in many countries – the parents look after the child for the first twenty years; then, for the next twenty, the child looks after the parents. If a couple has a girl, when she marries she will become part of her husband's family, and her parents will have no one to look after them in their old age if she is their only child. The solution for all too many was to abandon daughters into the care of the state.

Back in the UK, I would always favour a solution that placed any child within its own birth family, if that was at all possible. But because abandoning a child was illegal in China, replacement with the birth family was never an option: the biological parents were long gone. Thus, the scheme we were implementing was the best hope for this abandoned generation.

The government did, in time, amend the one-child policy, in an attempt to address this issue. In 2002 it launched a 'Love Girls' campaign, which meant if the first child of rural parents was a girl they were allowed to have another baby. If a second child was also a girl, then the state would build the family a small house as a reward (and to prevent illegal infanticide). The one-child policy went through other permutations, with qualifications to the one-child limit in various circumstances, but it remained in force right up until 2016, when it was finally dropped.

While we had been steadily progressing our scheme, our ally, Sir Richard Branson, had not been idle since that meeting in London in the spring of 1997. True to his commitment to us, he had launched a fundraising campaign on Virgin Atlantic's international flights, which he called Change for Children. There was even a music video for which Whitney Houston had donated the use of her song 'Step by Step'. Through this campaign, Virgin had managed to raise more than £60,000 for the orphans of China, which had been a welcome supplement to the money we were getting from DFID once that funding had finally come through.

Towards the end of 1999, we passed our first big milestone, having placed more than a hundred children with families around Shanghai and its outlying districts. Richard Branson offered to mark it with a special celebration in the Shangri-La Hotel in central Shanghai, and invited every one of the first hundred families. He was quite savvy in the way he went about it. He didn't make a song and dance, and no press or media were invited. The evening was only for the families, and a few judiciously chosen Chinese officials. The message was clear: Virgin Atlantic was here to help the Chinese people and was not simply out to get what it could. I thought that was quite smart, since it won him and his business a lot of goodwill among the officialdom of Shanghai.

'Roger!' he cried, weaving his way through the crowd towards me. 'Congratulations!'

'Hello, Richard,' I said, once more overlooking that he couldn't remember my name.

'One hundred families,' he grinned, clinking his champagne glass against mine. 'That's quite a number.'

'It's a start,' I said, nodding agreeably. 'But I want more.'

'How many?'

As many are the stars . . . I smiled. 'A lot more.'

A few days later, I received an email from Branson with the subject header 'Fly the Glovers home for Christmas'.

'We've won the route!' his email announced.

So, on the morning of Christmas Eve, the eight of us took our seats on the first direct flight from Shanghai to London. I leaned across to Liz. 'Not a bad Christmas, this one, eh?'

12: Gospel Living

Preach the gospel at all times. When necessary, use words.
(attributed to St Francis of Assisi)

As we settled into life in Beverley Hills, we began to find our stride. The children had a routine. I was working hard with the family placement project at the orphanage. Liz was making things work for the children, creating a haven, and building relationships with our friends in the village and elsewhere around the city.

But we hadn't come to China to feel secure. We wanted to make a difference, not only through our work but also through our lives. We wanted to love the Chinese people.

We had both spent time with Jackie Pullinger by now, and we had begun to pray that our eyes would be opened to the poor, so that we might be given the same passion for them that she had. We knew there were restrictions – quite tight ones at the time – on spreading the gospel, on telling Chinese people about Jesus, but we also knew that at the least we could 'be Jesus' to our neighbours, whoever they were and wherever we found them. As St Francis is famously believed to have said, 'Preach the gospel at all times. When necessary, use words.'

There were numerous examples of how a little act of kindness would open wide a person's heart, and Jesus would always enter in along with that gesture. Sometimes – not always, but sometimes – he would be recognised and received.

Not long after we had moved into Beverley Hills, we heard that a motorbike had run over a little boy in the village and left him with a badly damaged foot and ankle. Liz happened to see the child one day soon after. She saw that his bandage was filthy, and it was obvious that the wound was going to become infected.

(Remember Liz was a trained nurse.) She went to a chemist and bought some antiseptic bandages and cream, and then went over to the family's house to wash the wound. This touched the parents, who had no money to do this themselves. Liz invited them over to our house and then asked another friend to come who spoke Chinese to help translate.

We asked the couple about their lives. They told us they were from Anhui, the neighbouring province immediately to the west of Shanghai, which was very poor. Many economic migrants came from there to find work in Shanghai. The couple wanted to know about Jesus, and so we told them. And even though our translator was not a Christian, through her words this couple came to invite Jesus into their hearts.

A few weeks later, as we were buying vegetables from the local market, Liz noticed a family with a disabled child. This, we were coming to realise, was very unusual in China. Most families would abandon disabled children into the care of state orphanages, and the birth of a disabled child wouldn't be registered, thus leaving the couple free to have another baby. It didn't take long for Liz to befriend this couple, too, and their son, Xiao. He was about ten years old and had severe cerebral palsy. He was often kept inside their cramped, dingy home because he couldn't walk. Like most of the villagers, this couple were poor farmers who had migrated to the city for a better life. But I was so impressed with the family, that they had chosen the harder path of keeping their disabled boy, that I kept saying to them in my broken Chinese, 'You are very good father. You are very good mother.'

We became friends. One day I was taking a little walk and I decided to drop in on them. I found Xiao alone. His parents were out in the fields and had left him strapped to a chair on some cushions. The tough reality was that they had no choice. They had no money to pay anyone else to look after him, and they both had to work to earn enough just to live. While they were out, he had slipped down on his seat and was hanging awkwardly, half on the chair, half on the ground, and he was clearly in pain. I rushed in to lift him up, thinking there had to be something we could do to help them.

After speaking to Liz and the children, we decided we would invest in Xiao. First, we bought him a pushchair so his parents could wheel him around the village. Then, during one of my trips to England, I must have mentioned him and his predicament, because a friend of mine said he could get hold of a specialist chair for disabled people. When he described it, it sounded just the job, with a push button that could turn the chair into a bed in a few seconds. There was only one problem: how to ship the thing out to Shanghai. A phone call later and Virgin Atlantic came to the rescue, offering to fly it out for us free of charge. It was a joy to see Xiao perched happily on his new electric chair sitting out in the sunshine, watching the other children playing football, with a huge grin on his face.

The decision to help Xiao actually caused some consternation in the village. They couldn't understand why a family of white westerners would go out of their way to help this poor family. That's just not what white foreigners do. When some of them asked why we were helping Xiao and his family, we explained that we were Christians, that we love Jesus and that he loves them. 'Because of that, we want to help.'

Whatever they made of that, it certainly changed the general view of us. They began to adopt us into their community. They brought meals round for us and hailed us in the street with a friendly, 'Ni hao!'

On another occasion, Liz and I had just put our own children to bed. As I looked out of the window, I noticed a family huddled together under a tarpaulin, draped in the lee of the Beverley Hills wall. It was cold and pouring with rain, and there was no way their covering would be able to keep them dry. I went to bed but struggled to sleep. I felt so troubled that any family should have to live that way.

The next morning, I went out to speak to them. They were

another poor family from Anhui. The father couldn't read and their twelve-year-old daughter was not in school. They had only recently migrated into the city and they had got absolutely no traction as yet. They were, more or less, destitute.

I spoke to a friend in the village and he agreed to let the family live in one end of his barns. It wasn't a permanent solution, but it was a start. I knew we had to find them something to do, some purpose that would give them a little bit of income. I wondered if the answer might be chickens. We'd kept them in Guernsey, and they had been a regular source of food for us and income for the children. So, the same day, I went out and bought the family five hens and a cockerel, the idea being that they could sell eggs. We helped them build a small pen for the hens, and by the end of day everyone was happy.

But that night, I still couldn't sleep.

I was thinking about the chickens. I knew that chickens don't lay if they've been moved. In fact, it usually takes a couple of weeks for them to settle down. I imagined how hungry that family must be . . .

'Where are you going?' croaked Liz, as I got up out of bed.

'If those chickens don't lay some eggs,' I declared, like some prophet of doom, 'the family won't last a day.'

I ran down to our fridge and grabbed a box of eggs, then snuck outside, through the gate and into the village. I crept through the darkness till I came to the chicken pen and, with great delicacy, not wanting them to kick up a fuss, I lifted each of the five hens and placed an egg underneath. Then I hurried back to bed.

When the mother showed me her five gleaming eggs that had been 'laid' in the night, beaming from ear to ear, I thought I'd pulled off the perfect crime. 'You'd better eat a couple and sell the other three,' I told her, which she duly did. I repeated my 'crime' every night for the next two weeks, just to be certain that they had enough produce to get their little business up and running.

They soon had quite the reputation in the village for producing the most delicious eggs, which was no wonder since they came straight from the supermarket. To this day, I don't know whether they were on to my ruse from day one and just pretended not to know in order to play me for a fool. Either way, I don't suppose it matters.

They had told me they were Christians, as were a lot of the migrants coming in from Anhui, which was known among the Chinese as the 'Jesus Nest'. Seeing that their daughter wasn't in school, I asked them whether I could get her a Bible to read, knowing that they could never afford to buy one. They readily agreed, so away I went and got hold of one.

I returned a few days later with the Bible tucked away under my armpit. In those days we weren't allowed to evangelise, and I wanted to be discreet, not wishing to upset Lao Yu, the village elder, or the other villagers by crossing that line. My pretext for coming to the village that particular evening was to coach the local youngsters at football. We had erected some goalposts on a patch of wasteland on the edge of the village and my children and many of the locals would come and have a kickabout once a week, and usually other folk would come to watch as well.

Quite a crowd had gathered, at which point the mother came up to me and demanded – in a voice so loud that the people back in her home province of Anhui could have heard it – whether I had her Bible yet. I did – it was buried in my kit – but my heart sank, and I dreaded what the response of the other villagers would be now that my cover on this little operation had been blown. But the mother didn't care about that, she was so eager to read it.

To my surprise, one of the others piped up, 'Can I have one too?', and then another said the same, and another. It was the last reaction I was expecting, but I think what many of the villagers had seen in us when we helped Xiao meant that they were curious rather than offended. It had gone some way to preparing the ground. Before long I had agreed to get them *all* their own Bibles. And as soon as I could, I did.

So I was learning by doing, discovering that when you begin by building a relationship with someone and then you meet their need, they become more receptive to the gospel. And when they receive it, God willing, their hearts are changed.

These are just some examples. I could list many more. But all of them show that we weren't doing anything particularly difficult. Buying bandages, washing feet, finding a child a wheelchair and buying a few chickens aren't complicated actions. If *we* could help these people, then anyone could. But it takes a heart ready to reach out and help. And, I suppose, a little bit of courage.

During those first couple of years we felt as though, as a family, we were existing in a kind of 'Holy Spirit bubble'. After our time of preparation in Guernsey, the hand of God was on us and we felt his favour, but we still prayed all the time.

Soon after we had arrived in Guernsey, Liz and I had started praying for God to use us, to use our family. If we encountered difficulties or had a significant need, then we would of course pray about that. But after we arrived in China, our prayer life became all-consuming. We were inducted into a life of total prayer – where prayer became as basic and essential as breathing – which we never would have discovered had we stayed in England. We had to live like this, since we knew we needed God in every part of our daily lives. Prayer for getting money, for travelling about the city, for provision for housing, for our basic utilities to be working, for the health of every single one of us from dodgy food or the poor sanitation around the city – every moment of every day carried risk, and we wanted God to be with us in all of it. But even though we knew that he was, not everything went according to plan.

At the orphanage, the boy who had captained the Shanghai Canaries football team to victory stayed on to work for me once he was old enough to leave. He proved to be a good assistant, and he was smart. But one day, I had been to the bank to draw out some of the money that Care for Children had wired over to us, itself the work of an entire day in order to navigate the endless carousel of bank tellers just to get the necessary sign-off to receive any funds. A silly lapse of attention meant that, in the evening, I jumped into my driver's car and left behind thirty thousand RMB (about US$3,000) in the top drawer of the desk in my office. I was only too aware that the lad knew that was where I kept a substantial amount of cash on any day after I had been to the bank. I got my driver, Kong Ming, to turn around.

I couldn't have been separated from the money for more than half an hour or so, and when I got to my desk I found the same stacks of notes, all bound up nicely. But when I counted the money, some was missing. I realised he had been quite subtle. He had removed just a few notes from each bundle, and by the time I returned he had already fenced it to someone else on the nearby Pu Yu Xi Lù.

I spoke to Mr Li about it. Obviously, the boy couldn't work for me any more, and he didn't seem very contrite when confronted with the theft. Mr Li decided not to discipline him – he didn't want to draw attention to what had happened – but he did move him to another role.

The incident left a sour taste in my mouth, not because this boy had stolen the money; had it been mine, I might have over-looked it, but I couldn't, because the money belonged to Care for Children and I had to account for every penny of it. No, the sour taste came from a feeling of guilt that I had laid such a big temp-tation in this lad's path and he had fallen right into it.

Besides this, we all got sick at one time or another, usually with a stomach bug from something we had eaten. I fell very ill a couple of years into our time in Shanghai, in January 2000. After some persuasion, the civil authorities had granted special permis-sion to hold the first public baptisms of foreigners since 1945. It was therefore a big deal for the church. The baptisms were to be performed in the church of Muen Tong on the People's Square in Shanghai. They were to be baptisms by full immersion, and the little plunge-pool we were using had been filled from a nearby fire hydrant. The water was anything but clean, and very close to freezing. As one of the elders of the International Church, I was chosen to do the dunking, which meant standing in this pool of freezing-cold water with wet clothes for a very long time. Each baptismal candidate had the opportunity to give their testimony to the assembled congregation. There was one Dutch fellow who spoke for twenty-five minutes. By the end of his long speech, I think most of the folk gathered were watching me in the plunge-pool rather than him, as my face turned several shades of blue.

I was wiped out after that, not from the cold in the end, but from the Giardia – parasites – that were in the water. The Chinese doctors put me on a course of very strong antibiotics to deal with a severe bout of giardiasis, but weeks later I was still very ill. It was so bad I had to fly home to England as none of the doctors in China could figure out why I wasn't improving. Finally, back in the UK, the doctor told me it was now the strong antibiotics that were the problem, not the infection. So I stopped taking them, and sure enough my health soon returned to normal.

There were other problems, ranging from the comic – Liz opening the cupboard in a friend's house to find herself face to face with a rat, calmly munching its way through some biscuits and completely unfazed by Liz's presence – to the absurd – Liz having to sketch the King's Tower, which was near the first place we lived in Shanghai, that being the only way she could get the taxi driver to understand where she wanted to go. And there were moments when even we had cause to doubt why we had come.

Perhaps the worst of these came about a year and a half after our arrival. Liz and I were sitting down at the kitchen table after the children were all in bed. I could see something was on her mind.

'What is it, love?' I asked.

She looked up. There were tears in her eyes.

'Tell me.'

'I don't think I can,' she said.

'Go on.'

She let out a big sigh. 'It's the children. I think we've made a mistake bringing them here.'

'What? The children are fine. They love it here.'

'I know they do – but what about their education?'

'They've all got school. They're learning Chinese–'

'But it's not what they had, is it? Guernsey was great for them. They had good schools and gangs of friends.' She shook her head, perhaps not sure what she wanted to say. 'What they're learning here, it's basic. It's not even that. It's awful. Come on, Robert, let's not kid ourselves. How are they going to get on in life if they haven't had a proper education?'

'They don't need to "get on",' I replied, a little too moodily. 'They need faith.'

We went to bed at an impasse. I had no idea this sort of thing had been bothering her. Soon enough I had fallen asleep, while Liz lay there in the darkness, her worries tumbling over and over in her mind. She was in a panic. Maybe it was a spiritual attack, I don't know, but I certainly didn't see things that way at all.

She told me the next day that while she was lying there she cried out to God in her heart to help her. And, still unable to sleep, she got up, went downstairs, opened her Bible on the table and began to read. The Old Book had fallen open at the second chapter of John's Gospel. On one leaf, she remembers, there was a map, and on the other the description of Jesus' first miracle, the wedding at Cana where he turned water into wine. As she read the passage, these words whispered in her mind: 'You see? Jesus took six clay pots and filled them with the best wine.'

At once, she thought of her own six little pots. Then she fell to her knees. 'I'm so sorry, God, I'm so sorry,' she said over and over. 'What am I doing?' she thought. 'My children don't need what the world has to offer them. They need Jesus to fill them.'

She thought about how we had left everything behind and come to China, how God had planned it all. And she felt him whisper in reply, 'That's right. Let Jesus fill them. That's all they need.'

In the morning, she was full of faith again, and full of praise to God that he was going to take our six precious clay pots and fill them with the best wine.

Only a few days after this, we were walking down the street as a family in central Shanghai. They always say, in Shanghai look down for the poverty and look up for the wealth. Well, even though we were in a wealthy district, you would still see beggars on the street corners. Suddenly one of our boys, Joshua – who couldn't have been more than six at the time – blurted out that he'd be back in a second and then took off across the street. We watched him approach a small girl walking barefoot along the pavement. He tapped her on the shoulder and she stopped. Then he took off his shoes and pressed them into her hands. For a moment she didn't understand, but, seeing his sincerity, she was soon thanking him.

'There you are,' I muttered to Liz, my heart nearly bursting with pride, 'they don't teach you that in school.'

But perhaps the most remarkable illustration of how a small act of kindness can bring about total transformation was this last story. It has left an indelible impression on my heart.

Mr Li had arranged for me to have a driver, Kong Ming. He was something of a diamond in the rough, but he was very reliable. He was driving me to work one morning along the expressway as usual, when I noticed a little man huddled on the side of the hard shoulder.

'Kong Ming,' I said, 'go back. We need to help that man.'

'No, *Lao Ban*,' he protested over his shoulder (*Lao Ban* means 'boss'), 'he can't come in car. He will have fleas and make car dirty.'

'Kong Ming,' I growled, filling his rear-view mirror, 'I said, go *back*!'

This time he grudgingly acquiesced and took the next exit to make our way back to the man, shooting sour glances at me in the mirror all the way.

We drew up alongside the man. I opened the door and called

out to him to get in. He got wearily to his feet. His hair was long and matted into thick ropes; his face was covered in black, oily grime so that you could hardly see any natural skin colour at all; his clothes were little more than filthy rags. As he climbed in, reeking like a garbage bin, I saw he was clutching a little bag of sunflower seeds, or 'idiot seeds' as they are sometimes known. He eased himself back in the seat next to me and immediately started spitting out the empty seed shells into the footwell, much to the disgust of Kong Ming who would have to clear them up later. I told Kong Ming not to worry about that and just to drive on to the orphanage, but I wasn't sure what we would do with our passenger when we got there.

When we arrived, I led him up to my office, where the other staff greeted him with utter horror.

'You can't bring this person in here!' Mrs Wong shrieked. 'This is quite wrong. I will call the police. They must deal with him. He is a vagrant.'

I tried to remonstrate with her, arguing that we should be caring for the man, not putting him in the hands of the law. But she wasn't having any of it, so finally I had to give in.

'Fine,' I conceded, 'but if he must leave, first we're going to give him some food, a wash and some new clothes.'

Reluctantly, Mrs Wong agreed to this compromise. I called Liz at home, explained the situation and asked her to bring over some clothes that might fit the man as quickly as she could. Meanwhile, one of the other staff took him to the shower block for his wash.

Twenty minutes later, the pair walked back into the office. Everyone stopped in their tracks. In the place of the bedraggled vagrant there now stood a beautiful young woman with a tumble of gleaming black hair and bright, rosy cheeks. The transformation was staggering. We were all struck dumb, but eventually people started to react. The difference in the staff's attitude to her was like night and day. Suddenly everyone was falling over themselves to be kind to her, to speak gently with her, to offer her food and refreshments.

Once she had eaten something, a couple of the staff sat down and interviewed her. Afterwards they told me her story.

She had come to Shanghai from the far-off province of Gansu, having heard that the city was booming and that she was sure to make her fortune. But when she arrived, the reality was very different from her dream. She couldn't find a job, no one offered to help her, and she was soon homeless and without a penny in her pocket. Destitute, there was no way she could go back home, even though her parents might be able to look after her, because to turn up at home in her beggared condition would have brought a terrible loss of face to her parents. It is hard for a westerner to grasp the importance of the concept of 'face', but it is core to Chinese culture. Such failure in full view of her parents' community would have been a huge dishonour to them; the shame would have stuck for ever. If she ever were to go home, the only way to keep face would be to bring gifts for all her family members and to look the part – in other words, wearing clothes that indicated some sort of affluence.

We decided to help her.

Liz and I had a couple of glass vases mounted in velvet boxes, which had been gifts from some event or other and which we were only too glad to give to her. We bought her new clothes and Rachel, our eldest, gave up some of her pretty hair clips. We booked her a train ticket back to Gansu province in a hard sleeper compartment (actually the second-best ticket type available) so that she could travel the long distance home in comfort. Liz and I took her to the station and saw her on to the train. As the train started pulling away, she waved to us, beaming like a child, a completely different person from the ragged creature I had found on the side of the expressway.

When I think of that beautiful young woman, for me, that *is* the gospel story. God finds us languishing in the filthy rags of our self-righteousness, dirty and wretched in our sin and shame. We have no honour. We have lost face. We cannot go home. Yet God welcomes us in, wretched as we are. He cleanses us, washes us clean of our filth and uncovers the hidden beauty inside us. He clothes us, raises us up, gives us gifts and pays the price for us to be restored to our true family. He calls us home. Shame turns to honour. Mourning turns to joy. Despair turns to hope.

We have the privilege of loving others because he first loved us.

13: Digging for Water

*And my God will meet all your needs according
to the riches of his glory in Christ Jesus.*
(Philippians 4:19)

The new millennium dawned, full of hope.

Richard Branson's Virgin Atlantic was flying direct to Shanghai,
Care for Children was well into its three-year partnership with
DFID, the Shanghai Civil Affairs Bureau was starting to see
tangible results from our placement programme, and as a family
we were feeling we belonged in this city.

That was all good. But there was still a niggle in my mind that
I returned to again and again: the promise that God had made
me. *You will be father to as many children as there are stars in
the sky.* More than I could count. Well, so far we had placed about
two hundred children in and around Shanghai, and even I can
count to two hundred. Yet there was a figure that kept popping
up in my head.

A million, a million . . .

It became a refrain that wouldn't go away, and so I started to
believe that perhaps that was the number God was aiming for as
well.

One million orphans placed in families across China.

That's quite a vision, I thought. It seemed impossible. Absurd.
In any case, the official statistics had the total number of orphans
in China at something like five hundred thousand.

I guarded this figure of a million closely in my heart. It was
only in early 2000, at a Care for Children board meeting back in
England, that I shared it with my fellow trustees for the first
time.

'You'd better not make that public,' said Richard Graham in his cut-glass drawl.

'Why not?' I asked.

'Because we'll be had up under the Trade Descriptions Act,' he laughed. 'There's no way we can deliver on a million.'

'It might look that way right now,' I said, once the laughter around the table had died away. 'Look,' I admitted, 'I don't know how it is going to happen. It might not even happen in my life-time. But if God says he will do it, he'll do it.'

My contract with Mr Shí and the Shanghai Civil Affairs Bureau required me, in addition to my other duties, to organise a biannual conference as well as annual workshops, in partnership with the Bureau. So, in July 2000, Care for Children and the Shanghai Civil Affairs Bureau hosted the first ever National Childcare Conference in the Shangri-La Hotel in downtown Shanghai. The intent was to share the vision for family placement with other social service leaders from around the country, and also to publicise what we had already learned in Shanghai. My fondest hope and prayer was to see the same programme we were running in Shanghai replicated in every province and every major city across China.

Lord Laming – a former chief inspector of social services whom DFID had asked for advice in regard to Care for Children – flew in from London to give the keynote address. At first he had been sceptical of me, wondering how much impact a man with little experience of China and almost no Mandarin language skills could have. But eventually he was convinced, and few have given greater support than he. Over the course of his involvement with Care for Children, Lord Laming became not only my professional mentor but also a close personal friend for whom I have the utmost respect.

Felicity Collier, Director of British Association for Adoption and Fostering, also spoke at this first conference, giving a ringing endorsement to our programme. And, more importantly, repre-sentatives from 135 Civil Affairs Bureaux around China, together with sixty-five other child welfare organisations, attended.

The conference was progressing well. We had left space in the agenda for an open forum, during which any delegates could stand up and share their thoughts, ideas and experiences, whether from inside China or overseas. The discussion turned to the total number of orphans in residential care in China.

This was the first moment I heard Yan Mingfu speak.

He got to his feet, a venerable old gentleman with salt-and-pepper hair and wearing a light-grey suit. Immediately, everyone around him fell silent. It was obvious from the other delegates' reaction that here was one of the most important people in the room.

'The figure that the Bureau of National Statistics has provided to the Ministry of Civil Affairs is five hundred thousand.' He paused and slowly removed his spectacles. 'I believe the true figure is closer to two million. So there is much work to do. I see no good reason why we need parents from other countries to adopt Chinese children. One day, I hope, it will be the people of China who will look after their own.' He then sat down. The flow of discussion continued.

When the session came to an end, I went to talk with him in person. I knew Yan Mingfu was Minister of Civil Affairs for the whole country, and, of course, I had known he was coming to the conference, but this was the first time I had spoken to him directly.

'That's an interesting figure, Mr Yan,' I said. 'Two million.'

'In my estimation,' he nodded humbly.

'What sort of impact do you think a programme like ours could have on that number?'

His lips pursed in a half-smile. 'If you mean how many of those could we place within Chinese families . . .' he thought about it for a few moments, '. . . I think 50 per cent is achievable.'

I stretched out my hand. 'One million, then,' I said.

He smiled and took it. 'Yes. I would like to see that.' We shook on it. And the number was sealed.

One very positive step forward which we had achieved in time for that first conference was an independent evaluation of the

Jimmy with his two
brothers 1972

HMS *Oberon* 1977

Wedding of Robert and Elizabeth
at Weybourne Church, Norfolk
14 April 1984

Pu Yu Xi Lu, Shanghai the
road of the Shanghai Social
Welfare Institution 1998

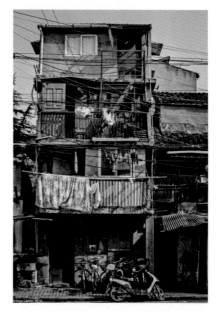

Signing ceremony with
the Shanghai Social
Welfare Institution
September 1998

Little girl with Robert, one of
the first to receive a family 1999

The Shanghai
Canaries 1999

Richard Branson visits
Robert in Shanghai 1999

The painting given to Robert by
a young Chinese artist 1999

Robert and Elizabeth after receiving
the White Magnolia Award from the
Mayor of Shanghai

Meeting with Maneka Gandhi,
Indian Minister of Social
Justice and Empowerment
in New Delhi 2000

Robert with Yan Mingfu, Minister
of Civil Affairs toasting the success
of Shanghai winning the Special
Olympics in London

Robert meeting Mr Wanlop
Phloytabtim, Permanent
Secretary of the Ministry of
Social Welfare in Bangkok,
Thailand 2003

Sun Yuan Jie with Robert and
Elizabeth at the Great People's
Hall, Beijing 2004

HRH Prince
Michael, the British
Ambassador to
Thailand and Robert
with the Generals of
the Thai Army

Robert receiving the OBE from HM
the Queen at Buckingham Palace 2005

Zhang Ziyi, the famous Chinese actress featured in *Crouching Tiger, Hidden Dragon*, Care for Children Ambassador 2007

Robert and Elizabeth at Capital M, Beijing 2007

The first ever Paralympian at the 2008 London Olympics from the DPRK

The staff at the Chengdu orphanage stand together in three minutes silence following the Sichuan earthquake in 2008

Robert's friend in Deyang orphanage who broke his ankles when he jumped with children in his arms from the third floor 2008

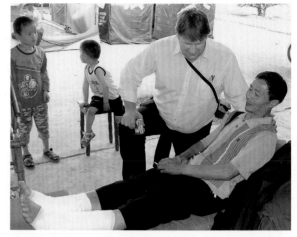

Thai delegation in London 2015

Francis Chan and Robert in Hong Kong 2017

Robert with Lord Laming, Phill Gray, YJ Sun in Phnom Penh, Cambodia 2017

Glover family
2017

The start of the Vietnam
project in Hanoi 2017

The opening of the Community
Centre in Yunnan, China 2018

Robert interviewing Care
for Children Global
Ambassador Bear Grylls in
Hong Kong 2018

Dr Shi and Mr Li

Robert and Lord Laming
return to Shanghai
to meet Dr Shi and
Mrs Gao 2018

The launch of
the documentary
Children of Shanghai
Hong Kong 2019

project in Shanghai. In early 2000, we decided to invite the Centre for Research on Children and Families at the University of East Anglia (UEA, based in Norwich) to carry out the evaluation, hoping it would show a clear advantage of family placement over residential care. So, in May 2000, just before the conference, Dr Chris Beckett from Cambridge University, Drs Shen and Zheng from East China Normal University, and Professor June Thoburn, Dean of Social Work at UEA, visited the orphanage to gather information and write reports on their findings.

They met and interviewed a foster family on the programme, spoke to teachers, went to support groups set up for foster carers, witnessed the care arrangements at the children's welfare centre, examined files and read background documentation. It was a full audit, in effect. Last of all, they met with Mr Shí, as Director of Shanghai Civil Affairs, and his subordinate, Mr Li, the Director of Shanghai Social Services.

Their conclusions were deeply gratifying:

The project is undoubtedly an impressive achievement on a number of grounds: the number of placements achieved in a short time, the number of foster-parents recruited (and the interest generated). The stability of placements for children who are generally considered 'hard to place' and 'hard to parent'. [Our placement failure rate was only 7 per cent out of all placements; a far lower number than was ever expected in the UK.] The diversity of placements. The creative interplay of British and Chinese experience, and the observed benefits to many of the children, who have progressed rapidly since moving from institutional care to foster-care.*

This independent evaluation earned us a lot of credibility with both the British and the Chinese governments. In fact, much to

---

* 'Shanghai Foster Care Project Evaluation', May 2000, conducted by Professor June Thoburn, University of East Anglia, and Dr Chris Beck, University of Cambridge, on behalf of the Department for International Development, UK Government.

my surprise, as a result of this the Mayor of Shanghai presented me with the White Magnolia Award, an accolade usually reserved for business people bringing commerce or investment into China. I was, of course, touched by the honour, but, more importantly, I was encouraged that, with this report, we had something substantial to show the other provincial administrations around China to demonstrate that the programme worked. We had a proof of concept, in effect.

The first representatives outside of Shanghai to show real interest were from Kunming, the provincial capital of Yunnan, in the far south of China. But up until the tail end of the year 2000, any planning with them was limited to a few calls back and forth, with the main point of contact being a lady called Madame Zhou.

Excited as I was at the prospect of Care for Children's work expanding beyond Shanghai for the first time, any thought of expansion immediately threw up the question of funding. Our arrangement with DFID was for three years only, which would run to the middle of 2001. DFID's intention from the outset had always been to provide seed funding for us in order to kick-start the project, although I had hoped, given its success, that it would want to continue funding us. However, when I welcomed the DFID man sent out to Shanghai to meet with us to discuss the plans 'going forward', I had a bad feeling in my gut.

'The project has undoubtedly been a great success,' he began, encouragingly enough, 'but Shanghai is an affluent city . . .'

'So?' I replied.

'Well,' he shifted awkwardly on his seat, 'the feeling is that the model won't work elsewhere in China. Not in the poorer, western provinces, certainly.'

'Why not? The programmes needn't cost that much, in absolute terms,' I said. 'It's just a case of finding willing parents, getting the local governments on side–'

'I'm sorry, Robert,' he cut in, with a weak smile. 'The bottom line is, we're not going to be renewing our funding.'

And that was that. I couldn't help wondering, if they were so concerned about the efficiency of their cost base, why they had bothered to fly their man all the way to China to tell me that.

It was a blow, certainly, but, nothing daunted, I went off to visit my great ally, Mr Shí.

'We need to take this outside Shanghai,' I said, brimming with enthusiasm for my vision of a million. 'Let's go into the cities in the west and the south. The orphanages there are already interested.'

He smiled at me, like a kindly uncle might at an over-exuberant child, and leaned back in his chair. 'No, no, Robert. We don't want to spread you too thin. We have plenty of work for you to do here in Shanghai.'

It seemed we had reached the limit of my patron's vision as well. He wasn't wrong, exactly. There was still plenty to be done in Shanghai. But until then, I hadn't grasped quite how parochial China could be. Government officialdom easily fractured into a myriad of petty fiefdoms, up and down the chain of command. Mr Shí was 100 per cent committed to Shanghai. Indeed, I knew he had passed up the chance to continue up the political ladder towards the higher rungs of the Communist Party in Beijing *because* of his commitment to Shanghai. So, in some ways, I shouldn't have been surprised by his damp response to my plans of expansion. Yet I couldn't shake that word spoken by the young girl in Guernsey: her picture of an Olympic torch being carried all over China, bringing light to many cities. I was sure that was what God wanted to do.

I now realised it was going to take a mind more expansive than Mr Shí's to help make that happen.

With the loss of the DFID funding on the near horizon, both we, the Glovers, and the other board members of Care for Children were coming under a lot of pressure regarding our expenditure. As an organisation we had committed to pay 150RMB per month to each family that took on a child, with the local government matching this with another 150RMB. For each family, this amount was sufficient to alleviate the additional costs of looking after a child, but it wasn't so much that they were making any money out of it.

It is interesting to note that many of the families refused the money. Instead, they were far more interested in the 'face' they stood to gain within their community. Each family that took on a child would receive a gold plaque from the Ministry of Civil Affairs, which declared, 'This is an honourable family . . .' and so on, explaining why they had received this mark of merit. The gold plaque was then affixed to the front of their house. Thus, the family's community would be able to see the high esteem in which they were held by the state. It was fascinating that while many families refused the subsidy, none of them refused the gold plaque.

By early 2001, we had placed five hundred children around Shanghai, two hundred more than the project's original target figure. We were committed to providing that money to these families for three years, but without DFID's funding there was no way we were going to be able to continue that level of support once it ran out. The stark reality was that, without this money, a proportion of those families would no longer be able to continue fostering. What would then happen to those children?

Liz and I began praying to God for a breakthrough. Meanwhile, we took action. We decided to organise a fundraising event in China for Care for Children. We wanted something dramatic that would catch the imagination, something iconic.

'What could be more iconic than the Great Wall of China?' suggested Rachel, when we put it to the children.

'What are you thinking?' I asked her. '"Walk the Wall", something like that?'

'Not the entire Wall, Dad, but maybe a section of it. I'm sure all sorts of people would love to do that.'

'All sorts of people' was certainly what we got. Twenty female social workers from the UK, five high-powered entrepreneurs from Shanghai (or 'weekend warriors' as some call them, who were frighteningly fit), an old friend from Sheringham ('old' in two senses of the word: he was in his seventies), another old friend, Peter Farley, who was in his sixties, and two hairdressers from Boston, UK. An eclectic bunch, to say the least.

It was an extraordinary experience, of course, and also a reasonable success. It raised twenty thousand pounds, which was good, but sadly wouldn't come close to replacing the DFID funding hole. But the trek is also worth mentioning for two episodes that occurred on it.

It was a six-day challenge, starting at a place called Mutianyu, about forty-five miles north of Beijing. The aim was to walk around fifteen miles a day, toiling up and down the sometimes staggeringly steep segments of Wall that tracked across the mountainous landscape of Hebei province, just outside the capital. The feat was no small ask of our participant fundraisers, and it didn't exactly get off to an auspicious start.

On the first day, one of the social workers fell ill – some sort of reaction to her vaccinations – and she had to be flown home. She had been waiting all her life to come to China, she said, and she was devastated. Before she left, I sat with her on the Wall while we waited for her transport to arrive, and I shared something of my story, much of which appears here on these pages. As we said goodbye, I offered to pray for her. She accepted and then off she went.

I thought nothing more of it. But a few months later I received a letter from her, saying she now understood why she had always wanted to come to China, and that reason had now been fulfilled. She explained that as I had shared my testimony with her and then prayed for her, she suddenly *knew* that Jesus was real. Upon her return to England, she had sought out a church and become a Christian, giving her life to Christ. She wrote, 'The reason God sent me to China was not to walk the Wall. It was to find Jesus.' For me, that alone made the whole endeavour of the trek worthwhile.

At the top of each hill summit, we were blessed with stunning views, shimmering below us through the spring haze, but hiking up and down those jagged hills was hard. By the evening of the fourth day, my friend Peter Farley's knee was a wreck. He slumped down next to me on a bench in the village we had just reached.

'How's the knee bearing up?' I said, offering him a swig from my water bottle.

'Pretty good agony, I don't mind telling you.'

'Sorry to hear that,' I said. 'You want me to pray for it?'

He shrugged. 'Sure.'

I put my hand on his bad knee and prayed a simple prayer, thanking God in faith for healing Peter's knee.

He gave a sudden snort of amazement. 'It actually feels better,' he said. He sprang up, laughing, and started to stretch his leg one way and then the other, and walked around to test its strength. 'It's completely better,' he exclaimed. 'There's no more pain at all!'

Although I had prayed for healing, I was still stunned by what appeared to be a small miracle.

Someone else then asked for prayer, since they were struggling, too. We prayed for them eagerly, feeling full of faith. I can't say they were healed of anything, but as God touched them they started laughing. Pretty soon we were all laughing, rolling around unable to stop. Seeing us like that, the villagers seemed to catch the mood and wanted to join in.

As the sun settled into the west, swathing the hillside in a golden light, the locals pulled out an almost unimaginable quantity of fireworks and began firing them up into the darkening sky. Further down the hillside, another village launched its own fireworks in answer, and the two went on and on like that until they must have blown up just about every incendiary object in the valley.

There was something magical about that night. It felt like joy spilling out of the heavens onto the earth below.

Twenty thousand pounds was not to be sniffed at, but it wasn't enough. We started having to tighten our belts. As a family, we moved out of our roomy house in Beverley Hills, first into an apartment development called Mandarin Gardens and then into an even smaller apartment on Hong Mei Lu. The first move was really because we wanted the children to move to another school near that location. The second, though, was because we didn't want there to be any question whether we were prepared to cut our cloth according to the funds available.

All the while, Liz and I continued to pray for God to provide us with all that we needed, and he never let us down. We were so sure that he would not have brought us this far, when everything was progressing so well with the placement project, to then let it all fizzle out to nothing.

A short while later, I received a message that three men were coming to visit me at the orphanage. When I opened the door to my office, I didn't recognise any of them. They were all ethnic Chinese but spoke perfect English.

'We've flown in from Singapore,' their spokesman began. 'Forgive us – I know you may find this strange – but we felt God tell us that we needed to come and pray for you.'

'You've come all the way from Singapore for that?' I was astonished, but, seeing their sincerity, I felt deeply humbled as well. 'Thank you,' was all I could think of to say.

When they offered nothing in reply, I began babbling to fill the silence, telling them all about the project, giving them statistics, the vision and all the rest. They took a polite interest in what I was saying, but they were not what I would call enthralled.

When eventually I paused for breath, one of the men said, 'Shall we pray then?'

'Yes,' I said. 'Yes, of course.'

So they did – nothing out of the ordinary, but honest, heartfelt prayers. And then, right at the end, one of them offered this. 'I see a picture in my mind. An image. It is of a big oak tree, with its roots sunk deep into the ground. But the water below has dried up, and the leaves on the tree are starting to die.' Now he really had my attention. 'I see more,' he continued. 'A big pond, not far away . . .' He nodded, his eyes closed, not wishing to speak before he had his words clear. 'I think you need to dig a channel from the oak tree to the pond, so the water from the pond can sustain the tree.'

It was a striking image, surely.

There had been so many images that had meant so much over the years, but this one remained an enigma for several days. However, I trusted that the answer would follow.

In fact, it came less than a week after these three mysterious gentlemen had left. This time my visitor was a lady from Hong Kong who was living in the US. She said she was impressed by our work and that she represented some charitable foundations in America.

'Would you be prepared to travel to the States to talk to these foundations about what you are doing in China?'

Even before she had finished the question, I knew in my heart that this was the 'big pond' that the man from Singapore had seen. It was time to dust off my shovel and start digging . . .

A few weeks later, I touched down in the United States for the first time in my life. From Washington DC I flew on to Tennessee, where I was to give a presentation to the board members and trustees of a large family foundation.

They gave me a thorough examination about the vision we had and the work we were doing. I suppose I could have been intimidated, but I believed so strongly in what we were doing and that God was in it, that I actually felt great confidence. I spoke about the family placement project, of course, but I also described how, as a family, God had broken our hearts for the poor and the homeless, and that we felt called to help them wherever we could.

'Well, hang on there, borrr!' exclaimed Tom, the grizzled patriarch of the family, in his southern drawl. He sat almost enthroned at the end of the long table. 'It sounds like you're torn between two visions there. So which is it? Are you helping the poor, or placing orphans in families?'

'Sir,' I said, drawing myself up to my full height, 'the vision and mission of Care for Children is to place children in families – which I believe is an open door to bring significant change to the nation of China. However,' I added, 'as a family and as Christians, we believe we cannot ignore the poor. If Jesus were here today, he wouldn't pass people by on the street, and so we won't either.'

Old daddy Tom looked at me and then around the table at some of the nodding heads of his kinsfolk.

'Oh-kay,' he drawled, his face cracking a wry smile. 'Would you care for some lunch, Robert?'

He took me out to one of those typical American diners I had seen in a hundred movies. I was still struggling to make sense of the place. The town seemed pretty scattered to me and I assumed where we were was somewhere on the outskirts of town. 'So where is downtown?' I asked by way of small talk.

'This is it!' boomed Tom.

'Oh . . .' I said, a little nonplussed. 'So what do people do around here?'

'Relocate,' commented the waitress as she slid our hamburgers and fries onto the table.

Whether it was truly as bad as all that, I don't know. But I, at least, was on the move. From Tennessee I went to Michigan, where I met Ron and Joyce and Joyce's amazing father, Paul. He reminded me of John Wayne – he would sit in his rocking chair on the porch and say, 'Robert, tell me about China.' Then we went on to Kansas, where Dave and Demi were the kindest people I have met. They would always think of the children back in China and were incredibly generous. From there I went to Newport Beach in California, where they told me it never rained; it's 'just sea mist'. Steve and his parents-in-law, Paul and Gail, were genuinely interested in what I was doing. In many ways, this meant more than the money they donated. Finally I travelled to Tacoma, up near Seattle in the north-west. Cary was a man of strategic thought who made such a difference.

Everywhere, I met with the boards of private family foundations. The individuals I encountered were some of the most godly, generous, warm-hearted people I have ever had the privilege to meet. Every single foundation I visited was to become a great supporter of our work in the years to come, and the people involved would become lifelong friends. I must also mention in this context David and Hollie and Chris and Susan in Tennessee.

The channel was dug. The funding was secure. And I returned to China filled with renewed confidence. The time had come to spread our wings and soar.

14: On Wings Like Eagles

_But those who hope in the L_ORD
will renew their strength.
They will soar on wings like eagles
(Isaiah 40:31)

They call it the City of Eternal Spring, and it is truly lovely.

Kunming is the capital of the southern province of Yunnan, where the temperature never drops below twenty degrees the whole year round. The air is clearer down there, the trees bright with rainbow colours, the mountains crowned with ethereal wreaths of cloud that give the place an almost mythical quality. It is little wonder that its landscapes are often the favourite subject of China's classical artists, as well as popular haunts for foreign backpackers and, in the twenty-first century, the swarms of domestic tourists who bus in from all over China.

But we were there for a different reason.

After my return from America, now standing on firmer financial ground, I went back to Mr Shí and explained the change in our position and restated my desire to expand the placement projects beyond Shanghai. I wanted his blessing, since it was thanks to him that we had come as far as we had. I didn't want to lose his patronage.

At last he agreed, but he impressed upon me the need to work in concert with the government channels in each province in order to keep the funding safe. 'Without them on your side,' he warned, 'it's wasted work.'

With his green light, I dialled up the communications that had already been ongoing with our friends in the south. It was soon agreed that we should send a small team, consisting of Mrs Lu, myself, Sunny and Priscilla (our training expert), down to Kunming to get things underway.

Our contact there was Madame Zhou, the Director of the Kunming State Orphanage, whom I had met at our National Childcare Conference in mid-2000. From the outset, she had been keen to see family placement happen in her province, and now we were in a strong position to help her. The four of us flew the two and a half thousand kilometres down there.

Madame Zhou welcomed us into her office and furnished each of us with a bowl of Monkey Oolong Tea – a speciality of Yunnan, so-named, she said, because in former times the tea plants sprouted off the side of mountain cliffs, and monks had trained monkeys to climb down the cliffs and pick the tea, so legend has it. As we sipped our tea, the discussions moved pretty fast. Madame Zhou had already identified a region called Tao Pu as a promising area to start. She explained it was one of the most rural parts of China.

'We want to start by placing two hundred children in one community,' she declared.

'Two hundred?!' I exclaimed. That seemed a staggeringly ambitious figure to me, even though I'd already been won round to the advantages of placing orphans in batches. But two hundred of them at once? 'Will that work, Madame Zhou?'

'We'll make it work,' she smiled.

I had to admire her hubris.

Later that same trip, we made the journey out to Tao Pu. It was a world away from the cosmopolitan whirl of Shanghai. The women in the villages we drove through were all attired in traditional ethnic dress; the men were stooped in paddy fields tending to their rice crop, their trousers rolled up to their knees. This was China in the raw. Even Mrs Lu and the others from Shanghai found it a tough environment.

On the last day of our visit in Tao Pu, they offered us a meal. Sometime around mid-morning, I heard a dog yelp, and then there was a strong smell of burned hair on the breeze. I followed the smell around the corner, thinking perhaps an outhouse or something had caught fire, only to see a couple of men blow-torching the fur off a dog for our lunch. The rural Chinese believe that dog meat keeps you warm in the winter, and – the brisk December air being rather cold – the staff proudly presented us with a bowl of dog stew a short while later. I ate it, but I can't say I ever developed a fondness for its strong, dark meat.

Everything arranged now, we returned to Shanghai. And then, a few days later, we sent back Mrs Lu and a staff member called Tony on a three-month assignment to kick off the project in Kunming, which meant interviewing potential placement families and training up the orphanage staff.

By now, Madame Zhou was becoming a firm friend. In the spirit of *guangxi*, she invited me and my family to visit them again for Chinese New Year a few weeks later. We were delighted to accept, only this time we would not be in Kunming, but vacationing with Madame Zhou and many of the other staff from her orphanage. (Remember how I said the Chinese often go on holidays with their work colleagues?)

Our initial destination was a city called Dali in central Yunnan. It was another paradise, only even more beautiful, even more serene than anything we had yet seen in China. For all of us, it was like a sort of honeymoon, and we fell in love with China all over again. Looming dark peaks rose up above green valleys, forming a backdrop to this city, which had once been capital to a smaller kingdom in the south of China before the Mongols overran it.

Dali was a two-day drive from Kunming, which we did in company with Madame Zhou and most of her staff. But even though it was long, it was magical.

The slopes beside the road were chequered with terraced paddy fields. The soil was a deep red and the woods and trees a deep green, despite the fact that it was technically still winter.

Liz kept the children entertained by reading to them, playing word games and telling stories. Sometime on the second day, Madame Zhou sat next to her. 'I always thought western mothers were terrible,' she said, 'but watching you with your children, I can see that I was wrong.'

That was quite an admission from a Chinese orphanage director. It was funny, because until then we hadn't ever thought of the Chinese people as watching us and judging our parenting, although we did know we were always a source of interest. With four blonde girls and blond twin boys, to the Chinese we were considered unusually fortunate.

Luck holds a great deal more currency in China than it does in the West. It's almost a tangible thing, which folk feel they can gain or lose by certain actions, or even acquire from another person considered especially fortunate. Of course, because of the one-child policy, to have healthy twin boys was considered the luckiest of all, and often poor Joshua and Joel had to put up with expectant mothers grabbing hold of them and rubbing their blond hair in the hope that they would give birth to twin boys as well.

As one of the ancient capitals of this part of China, Dali was full of historic buildings and architecture. Old, stone city walls broken by bright red-and-blue gatehouses, temples with swooping eaves and clay-tiled roofs, pagoda towers rising above the roof-tops, ornamental lakes and intricately manicured gardens, it was a tourist's dream. And with Chinese New Year in full swing, the sound of fireworks crackled throughout the city, and when the sun fell, bright explosions of red and yellow and green lit up the night.

Our children went off to play with the local children they had met, mainly to set off fireworks. As parents, now we had been in China a few years, this was something we had become extremely relaxed about. Liz, meanwhile, was ushered into a steamy kitchen that had been transformed into a full-scale dumpling factory, to help the other women prepare our feast. And I was taken off by the menfolk in our group, apparently with the sole intention of drinking huge quantities of *baijiu*, the white rice liqueur so potent that it burns your mouth, throat, stomach and anything else it comes into contact with. Chinese men adore it and, given even the slightest excuse, they will drink it in abundance.

I soon found myself trapped within an endless cycle of toasts, while the chatter grew ever more raucous and my head ever more giddy. I knew that, if I didn't come up with an excuse pretty quickly, this was all going to end rather badly. But since this was all an exercise in *guangxi*, I didn't want to cause offence by rejecting their hospitality, nor lose face by embarrassing myself. Suddenly it came to me in a flash of inspiration.

'I'm so sorry,' I announced. 'I'm afraid in England I would be considered a very bad father if I did not have all my children in bed by eight o'clock.' I checked my wristwatch and shook my head. 'I must get them back to the hotel.' They accepted my excuse graciously enough and wished me well. I made my escape, sweeping up Liz from the kitchen in a cloud of *baijiu* fumes, and herded the children into some semblance of order. Only one of them, Megan, had burned a hole in her jumper (thanks to a wayward firework). The fact that this was all the damage that had been suffered I considered to be a success.

I had to lean on Liz all the way back to the room.

From Dali, we drove further up into the mountains to Lijiang. By now we were approaching the foothills of the Himalayas and it felt as though we were entering a new and magical world. The little town was built up the side of a mountain, with cobbled streets lit by lanterns (admittedly that was thanks to a temporary power cut). A stream chuckled its way down through the old town, glowing with the candles that the locals floated on its surface to mark the auspicious time of year. It was freezing cold, but everywhere there were pots of heated coals, and we ate our dinner outside with one of these under the table to keep us warm. I can still picture looking around the table at the faces of my beautiful wife and children, each bathed in the warm gold of the candlelight.

But the dream wasn't yet over.

After a good night's sleep, we set off from Lijiang on horseback, heading up towards a huge ridgeline hanging above us. We were told that this was the edge of the great Tibetan plateau, and once we had climbed over it we would be visiting a small ethnic minority community called the JingPu, who lived up on the plateau about two hours' ride away.

As we climbed higher and higher, the sound of singing floated down to us through the mist. After we cleared the ridge, the path flattened out, and shortly after that we saw them, the whole community gathered together, singing in unison to welcome us. They were wearing fur hats and long crimson robes to keep out the cold, and broad smiles. The elders stepped forward to greet us and, that barely done, a snowball fight broke out between our children and some of the local boys and girls. At first, there were only four on their side, then six, then ten, then all the children joined in, scooping up handfuls of snow and pelting each other amid shrieks of laughter. I stepped into the fray and ran around chasing the Chinese children, growling like the big ogre they no doubt took me for.

Later, we all ate together in an open barn, sitting on crude wooden stumps for stools and eating off leaves for plates.

This journey affected our family deeply. Here we were in this remote corner of the vastness of China, at the tip of one of the outer tendrils of human life, far from the beating heart of a big metropolis like Shanghai or Beijing. But here, too, was love and friendship, community and joy.

As I looked around at the shining faces of our hosts, I had never been more convinced that what could be done in Shanghai could be done here, too. Wherever there were willing hearts ready to love them, children would be able to thrive.

Chengdu was next to rise.

This is the largest city situated in the central west of China, and the capital of Sichuan province. Sichuan is famous for its searingly hot cuisine, and also for its pandas – and, in 2008, for the earthquake that devastated so much of the province (of which more later).

The family placement project began a little differently from those in Shanghai and Kunming. Instead of sending out Chinese nationals to lay the foundations, our friends William and Nicky Lambert volunteered to go, working under the auspices of Care for Children. We knew them from Shanghai, where William had been working high up the ranks of Cable & Wireless. William was in his early forties and had become disillusioned with the expat life in Shanghai. He was looking for a life with more purpose (as so many high-flying and wealthy expat workers that we encountered in Shanghai were, although many never found much more purpose than fast living and making more money).

The Lamberts were Christians, from an evangelical background certainly – meaning they wanted to see the gospel spread throughout China – but they were less familiar with the charismatic and prophetic experiences we'd had, and the active (sometimes radical) approach we took to our faith. I think it's fair to say that they were struck by what they saw in us. To their credit, William took the bold decision to quit his high-paying corporate job in Shanghai and to commit, with Nicky, to spearheading the family placement project in Chengdu instead. They relocated there with their two sons and remained there for three years, until William's father died and they had to return to England. By then, they'd made a remarkable impact and had helped to place a very large number of orphans around the province of Sichuan. To this day, the Chengdu project remains one of Care for Children's biggest success stories.

By now, our format was becoming easily replicable – although always with an eye and an ear open to making whatever tweaks were necessary to accommodate local idiosyncrasies. The process began by hand-picking several orphanage staff members and training them to become family placement officers. William and Nicky went at it with such intent and energy that they soon became a source of encouragement to us in our own work back in Shanghai.

The Chengdu government put one of the orphanage workers, Tiang Yisu, in charge of the placement project (working hand in hand with the Lamberts), and she did so well that she was later appointed vice director of the orphanage. Within a few years, Tiang Yisu would become one of the leading experts on family care in China.

When I think of Chengdu, there is one child who encapsulates almost perfectly what we were doing. Li Li had been abandoned within days of her birth. When I first saw her, she was two years old and very sick, badly undernourished and thin as a reed. The doctors said she had a hole in her heart and was too weak to be considered for family placement, but we decided, on balance, that it was better to give her a family for whatever time she had left.

It was some time before I returned to Chengdu and saw Li Li again. The transformation was shocking, but wonderful. She was a different girl, now the picture of health, with round, pudgy cheeks, prancing around the room in a ballet costume. I was awestruck: her new mother's love had transformed her. It was the most visual confirmation to me of the theory that I had believed for so long. That transformation could never have happened inside an institution.

Li Li was now strong enough to have the operation on her heart to close the hole, but when she went for her initial tests in hospital, the consultant surgeon presented the results with tears in his eyes. There was no longer a hole in her heart. It had closed up. She no longer needed an operation. The story was picked up in the press and was splashed across the front page of several national papers: 'Miracle Baby Healed by a Mother's Love'.

It was no exaggeration.

One day, approaching Christmas in 2000, I arrived at my office to find a package awaiting me on my desk. I say 'package' – it looked like a crudely knocked-together pile of driftwood. Intrigued,

I unfastened the catch and opened up the lid. Inside was a beau-
tifully decorated porcelain plate, depicting a map of the province
of Ningxia. There was a note included. It read, 'May your God
bless you at this special time of year.' At the bottom of the note,
I saw the sender was a certain Lu Xiao Ping, an orphanage director
from the city of Yinchuan in Ningxia province in the north. She
had attended our first National Childcare Conference earlier in
the year.

Just then, Mrs Lu came into the room. 'What is that?' she asked.

'It's a sign,' I said, a smile creeping across my face.

'A sign? Meaning what?'

'That we're going to Ningxia.'

The gift was so unusual that I was certain it signified that an
open door awaited us in Yinchuan. And sure enough, the project
soon took root there, thanks in large part to Lu Xiao Ping's entre-
preneurial drive. In fact, she was so remarkable that she was later
named the nation's Woman of the Year – I think, in the second
year of the project – which gives you some idea of how fast she
got things moving there.

Ningxia is a dry, desert-like region in the centre north of the
country, a so-called autonomous region for the Hui people, an
ethnic group defined predominantly by their Muslim faith. The
landscape is epic and so is its history. This is Silk Road territory;
it lies just across the border from Mongolia, and was on the front
line when the Mongol hordes came pouring south. It was, of
course, from the west, along the Silk Road, that the Islamic influence had travelled, much more than a millennium ago. But history
continues to work its mark on the people of Ningxia.

A simple encounter with a potential placement family when
we were vetting candidates gave me a flash of insight into how
fast Ningxia was changing. We met the grandfather of the family,
who wore the traditional white hat of the Hui, a mark of his
commitment to his religion and ethnicity. He wore a Mao jacket,
he read his Qur'an and went to the mosque on Fridays. His son
owned a white hat but didn't wear it all the time. He wore what

I would call normal clothing – shirt and trousers, albeit a little old-fashioned, perhaps. He owned a Qur'an but didn't read it much. Occasionally he went to Friday prayers. His daughter, the third generation, wore the latest fashion items she could find in the local markets (always knock-offs of fashionable western brands). She didn't subscribe to the religion of her fathers, and nor did any of her friends. She didn't own a Qur'an. She never went to the mosque.

This progression – or dilution – summed up sixty years of history for me.

The Islamic population dispersed around China endures a hard time from the Communist Party authorities at the centre; some, but by no means all, of it is justified. My time in China was punctuated with incidents in the news of terrorism by insurgent groups (usually Islamist), rioting in the west of the country, flare-ups between ethnicities in different provinces. One of the government's policy responses to all this has been to move large numbers of Han Chinese (the majority ethnicity in China) into the big cities of the west. Yinchuan was one of these, and there has been a steady dilution of that province's Hui ethnicity for the last couple of decades. The same has been done in the biggest city in the far western province of Xinjiang, called Ürümqi, which even hit the international headlines in July 2009 on account of the violent clashes there between the indigenous Uighurs and the Han 'colonists'.

All this is by way of cultural and ethnic background, but it gives you some idea of the varieties in context that each new placement project faced and to which it often had to adapt. But whatever the context, it never altered the fact that giving orphans the chance to grow up in a loving family environment was significantly better for them than raising them in institutional care. In that sense, I believe it to be a universal truth. Family *is* God's plan for children.

By the end of 2001, we had projects running in Shanghai in the east, Kunming in the south, Chengdu in the west and Yinchuan in the north. There was some sense of completion in that, as if we had the four points of the compass covered.

But God wasn't done yet.

Not by a long way.

15: Angels Among Us

Do not forget to show hospitality to strangers, for by so doing
some people have shown hospitality to angels without knowing it.
(Hebrews 13:2)

Our time in Shanghai was approaching its end.

The three-year partnership with DFID ran out mid-2001. The arrangement with them had been that, apart from paying my salary, which amounted to around £18,000 a year, DFID would provide funding of 150RMB a month for every family in which an orphan was placed. I've already explained how we secured funding to replace the hole DFID left behind. We also had some success raising money in partnership with the British Chamber of Commerce, thanks in large part to the British Consul in Shanghai, Warren Townend, who proved to be a great advocate for the cause during our time there.

Because of this and our other sources, we were able to maintain our funding commitments to the families in Shanghai. As I've already mentioned, we exceeded the original target of three hundred and ended up placing more than five hundred orphans in families.

For Mr Shí, the project was a total success, but it had also reached its conclusion. To his mind, family care of orphans was never supposed to entirely replace institutional care or to render the orphanages obsolete. It was intended to offer a proven, positive alternative to residential care. And it had certainly done that.

Thus we celebrated the end of the Shanghai project in typical Chinese style sometime around the middle of 2002. There was a ceremony, awards were given and a lavish banquet was thrown for all involved, to which various grandees of the Shanghai political establishment were invited, as well as many key players from the Care for Children (or western) side, who had supported us in different ways.

After that, Mr Shí's active mind was already on to the next thing. The next time we met, he started talking about the elderly. 'There's no reason why we can't do something similar for them.'

But I had to pull back. Care for Children's vision was very clear: it was about orphans, not the elderly, or anyone else. And it was important to stay focused, particularly at this point, when the new cuttings in Kunming, Chengdu and Yinchuan were just being grafted in. It would have been easy to get distracted by other new projects in Shanghai.

However, a far greater distraction presented itself around this time.

I had just come out of a meeting in Shanghai when I received a message to return a phone call from New Delhi. My first thought was why on earth should I call anyone back in New Delhi? I didn't know anyone in New Delhi, nor did I have the spare money to be making expensive international calls to India.

In the end, my curiosity got the better of me.

'This is Robert Glover,' I said. 'I got a message to call you back.'

'Ah, Mr Glover,' answered a high, sing-song voice on the other end of the line. 'When are you coming to New Delhi, sir?'

'I'm not,' I growled. 'Who are you? What's this about?'

'Ah, of course, Mr Glover, waiting there, waiting there!'

I heard rapid footsteps click away into silence, and a few seconds later more clicks growing louder, then a woman's voice came on the line.

'Hello, Mr Glover.' Her voice was soft, but assured. 'We would like to invite you to New Delhi.' Before I could answer, she began to introduce herself. 'My name is Maneka Gandhi. I am Minister of State for Social Justice and Empowerment. We have heard of your work in China and – if I can be frank – we would like you to come and help in India.'

Well, that was a bit of a bombshell. And, I confess, it threw me. I'd had no sense of anticipation of this at all – but here I was speaking to a woman right at the top of India's government who was offering me an open door to come and help the children of her country.

Could this be a new direction? A new calling from God? Between them, China and India are home to one-third of the world's population. Was this how that prophetic word about the stars in the sky would be fulfilled?

I cobbled together a few questions of my own, but by the end of the call Mrs Gandhi had persuaded me to come and visit her in New Delhi.

'Is this you, God?' I prayed, as I put down the phone.

The day I arrived in New Delhi was a Sunday.

I felt horrible. Unusually for me, I was feeling the jet lag from the flight badly. My hosts had arranged for me to stay at the Sheriff of Bombay's house. But I felt so peculiar that, as soon as I had dropped my bags there, I went out for a walk around the district to clear my head. Even early in the morning, the air in the street was warm, dry and dusty. It was going to be a burning hot day before much longer.

I drifted along, rubber-necking the streets, until I came across an impressive building, gleaming white and with a fleet of mini-buses parked outside, each marked with a different sign: 'Youth', 'AIDS' and 'Medical Mission'. It was obviously a church, but judging from its resources, I thought, 'Wow, these people must be doing something right.'

As I gazed at the building, I noticed a man with leprosy sitting on the roadside beside the entrance to the church. Just then, a man pulled up on a motorbike and hopped off. He squatted down next to the man, peeled an orange and fed it to him segment by segment; then he gave him a few swigs from a tea flask, stoppered the lid, hopped back on his bike and sped off.

A short while later, the congregation began to arrive for the Sunday service. They were all smartly dressed and chattering away to each other. I watched from across the street as each one passed the man with leprosy. At first I was shocked, and then angry, that not one of them so much as looked at him. I had only just set foot in the country but for some reason this really incensed me. I had an urge to go and collar the priest, but thought it better to wait at least until after the service.

As I sat waiting, I scoured my Bible, asking God for a verse to share with the priest. Eventually the service ended, the people began to leave and I had my opportunity to speak with him. He was a small man, and I'm afraid my fury hadn't died down much.

'Is this a Christian church?' I asked in a gruff voice.

'Yes, sir. Yes, sir,' the priest replied, a little nervously.

'Then do you teach your flock how to care for the poor?' I demanded.

He shook his head sadly. 'Oh, sir, we are so blinded by the poor in this country that we no longer see them.'

I gave him the verse I had felt God had given to me: '"We should continue to remember the poor." Paul wrote that to the Galatians. Preach it next week,' I told him.

It occurred to me later that he might have interpreted this as being accompanied with a silent threat – 'Or else . . .!' – which hadn't been my intention. In any case, his head bobbed up and down as he fell over himself to say that yes, indeed, he would. Most certainly, he would.

After all I had seen in China, the injunctions of God that I found in the Bible were now non-negotiable. Of course, I understand that overwhelming poverty can have a paralysing effect on us. The deadening hand of despair. But I also know that when we reach out our hand, so too does God. And his hand is a lot stronger than ours. Doing nothing is not an option for the Church of Jesus.

This episode left a sour taste in my mouth: to see an entire congregation of Christians walking past a leper on their doorstep without so much as a glance; Christians playing the priest and the Levite and not the Samaritan.

Within a few hours, I realised that even I had never seen anything like the poverty that existed there.

On the Monday morning, a car arrived to drive me to Mrs Gandhi's offices. Driving along the streets and boulevards of New Delhi, I had never seen so many people in one place, and coming from China, that was saying something. The car nosed its way through the crowd at the gates of the Ministry building, all of them seemingly clamouring for a handout.

I was taken inside and shown into the atrium of Mrs Gandhi's office. She appeared on cue and ushered me into her rather grand ministerial office, sat me down opposite her and politely served me Indian tea and biscuits. She was a charming woman, evidently gifted with immense wisdom as well as a deep knowledge of and love for her country. We sat for some time, discussing the status of social welfare around India and, in particular, the welfare of the nation's orphans. The situation sounded challenging, to say the least.

Mrs Gandhi was quite straightforward to deal with. From the outset she was clear that she wanted me to partner with the Indian government, and to do what we had done and continued to do in China.

I made positive noises but no commitment. I realised how alien I felt in this country. I couldn't read people, had no instinct for what people wanted or how they were thinking. Looking back, I suppose that only shows all the more that my uncanny understanding of the Chinese people was a gift from God, appropriate to the purpose he had for me.

Despite my reservations, I allowed things to progress. Later that week, we travelled together to Mumbai and Mrs Gandhi took me to see the largest slum in the world. The world has seen it now, somewhat glamorised by the blockbuster film *Slumdog Millionaire*. But it was anything but glamorous to witness that level of poverty and degradation in the flesh. It broke my heart. I cried for three days after what I saw.

It occurred to me when I came away from India that, if nothing else, Communism has provided a safety net for the poorest of the Chinese people. Yes, individuals have slipped through but, by and large, the state doesn't abandon anyone if it can help it. People are not left to rot on the street in their filth and their squalor. But in India, everything seemed to fall through the net, and keep falling.

I still feel great sadness just thinking about it. It is the same as I felt during that week, the whole time I was there – heavy and oppressed, strangely sapped of energy and initiative. This was very different from the way I felt in China.

On the plane home, I prayed, wanting to hear from God. I just heard his gentle voice say, 'I didn't call you to India. Go and get on with the work I have given you to do.'

When I returned home, I told Liz all about what I had seen and what Mrs Gandhi and I had discussed. Despite what I thought I had heard from God, I still had doubts about what to do. Should I progress things? Was I, like those churchgoers, simply turning away when I should roll up my sleeves and step in? Was I a hypocrite?

For a short while, I still didn't rule out India, even though I sensed the country could easily become a blind alley into which Care for Children's work could run into a brick wall.

I did one more trip to India, and this time Liz came with me. Though she loved the vibrant colours and the warmth of the people, she too felt that it wasn't the right time to launch a project there. The door *was* wide open. And yet, without God's call, we dared not walk through it. On the other hand, he had spoken loud and clear to us about placing orphans in families in China. So we resolved that, until he told us otherwise, that is what we would do.

Meanwhile, I had been driving things forward with our three 'plants' from our base of operations in Shanghai. And every year we continued to hold our annual National Childcare Conference, which was steadily strengthening our profile and, more importantly, our relationships with other provincial government representatives around the country.

Already I was doing a lot of travelling. But I made a point of always being away from home for less than a week, so Liz could be sure I would be home on a Thursday night and that I would spend two or three solid days with her and the children before the next trip.

This travel wasn't like usual business travel. Wherever I went, I would step off the plane or the train and at once I would be met by some official (often in the military) and escorted to wherever I needed to get to. This was undoubtedly useful, if a little surprising. There was always mention of Yan Mingfu. You will remember him as the man with whom I had shaken hands over a mutual commitment to see one million orphans placed in family care.

Nothing was too much for 'a friend of Yan Mingfu', it seemed. His influence went before him and the fact that I was his friend opened up positive meetings and *guangxi*. It started to become clear to me that these open doors, and the energy with which the provincial authorities would mobilise their resources to help us, could only be the result of pressure from above. This was not necessarily aggressive pressure, but even a word from a man like Yan Mingfu carried more than sufficient weight to result in instant obedience from his subordinates, which meant almost everyone in China. I'd seen that in action myself.

I sometimes wonder what mires of corruption or bureaucracy we might have sunk into had we been attempting to expand our work from the grassroots up. Water runs downhill very quickly from the top of China's political mountain, but it's a hard grind to scale its sheer face from the bottom upwards. One quickly runs into the glass ceiling of each petty official's little fiefdom: an endless series of stop signs, each of which would require a little greasing of the cogs in order to advance to the next level, which a small charity like Care for Children simply wouldn't afford to do.

So, by this time, I was aware of Yan Mingfu's powerful influence in our favour. What I couldn't yet fathom was *why* he had swung in so firmly behind us? What was his motive? What did he hope to achieve?

It was towards the end of our time in Shanghai that I began to find out.

In the early summer of 2002, I had been invited to join Yan Mingfu for dinner in a restaurant perched high above the famous Bund district in Shanghai, looking out over the HuangPu river and across to the Pudong district, which was already almost unrecognisable from the marshy construction site it had been when we had first arrived four years earlier.

We were sitting outside on the terrace. There were a few other guests. The night was bright with the neon lights of the city. Yan Mingfu had permitted me to bring along a friend of my own, Fraser White, a man with a brain the size of a football. Fraser was one of the Shanghai businessmen who had walked the Great Wall with me. He had once been a senior partner at Clifford Chance, one of the world's biggest law firms, but, after sharing his vision for good education in China and a little encouragement, he gave up the law to run Dulwich College's global educational franchise. (It was still in its infancy back then; today it has sites all over the world.)

We were drinking a fine Bordeaux, a favourite of Yan Mingfu, and already we were two or three bottles down between us. One by one, the other guests said their goodbyes and left, until there was only myself, Fraser and Yan Mingfu, a translator and Yan Mingfu's assistant at the table. That was when things got interesting. Fraser began to ask questions, and Yan Mingfu began to answer them.

This was a man who had been with Mao, who had remained in his inner circle all the way through to Mao's death, who had weathered all that came afterwards – the Gang of Four had him locked up – and who had survived with his reputation intact, right up until the present day. He had come to international prominence during the Tiananmen Square crisis when, as a government minister and knowing that Li Peng was about to send in the tanks to disperse the protesters, he went to the students and offered himself as a hostage, his intention being that they would leave before the situation escalated even further. They turned him down and suffered the horrific consequences, but it had been a supremely brave act. Politically he fell out of favour for a while as a result, but, as a man, he remained enormously respected throughout China, and eventually rose up again under the premiership of Jiang Zemin. The people call him 'Uncle', and I can personally vouch for the powerful charisma he possesses

On this occasion, we were talking about his time with Mao. His was the mouth of history: alive, acutely intelligent and ready to talk. Fraser had all kinds of questions about Mao and I will relate only a few things here. But, to this day, it remains the most fascinating evening I ever had in China.

Yan Mingfu had been Chairman Mao Zedong's Russian translator during the height of his premiership, when the Cold War was at its most chilly and at a time when Sino–Russian diplomatic relations were of crucial importance to both states. Yan Mingfu, as a young man, was literally the mouthpiece between Mao and Khrushchev.

His first revelation was that Mao detested the Russians, even though they had to show the rest of the world that they stood in solidarity. But he hated them, and Khrushchev in particular. He couldn't stand the man, which often required some deft thinking on Yan Mingfu's part. He recalled one particularly fiery meeting at which Khrushchev removed his shoe in anger and banged it on the table to reinforce his point. Mao leaned back in his chair, instructing Yan Mingfu in a calm voice, 'Tell the honourable gentleman that if he does that again, we will come with our tanks to Moscow and we will burn it to the ground. Tell him that.'

Yan Mingfu turned to Khrushchev and, speaking Russian, said, 'You must understand, Honourable Chairman, that in Chinese culture it is very disrespectful to show the soles of your feet. Even to put your shoes on the table is disrespectful and Chairman Mao kindly asks you that you do not do this again.'

The next time Khrushchev visited Beijing was for a global convention of Communist Party politburos from around the world. Mao had arranged to have a bed for the Russian premier placed in the Temple of Heaven. 'It is the very highest honour,' Khrushchev was told. What he wasn't told was that there were no sides to the Temple of Heaven. It was the middle of summer, and Beijing was plagued with swarms of mosquitoes. The next day, when he addressed the three thousand Communist delegates, Khrushchev's normally pasty skin was blotched an angry scarlet, since he was covered head to toe with mosquito bites. Yan Mingfu's eyes twinkled behind his tortoiseshell glasses as he remembered how the Chinese delegates had all struggled to keep straight faces.

There were other occasions. Mao was a great swimmer, and he knew Khrushchev could not swim. So he always made sure one of the extracurricular activities of the Russian Premier's visits was a swim, and he enjoyed seeing Khrushchev's humiliation as he floated haplessly in a rubber ring.

Fraser and I had heard all the bad stuff about Mao, of course. But here we were, hearing a different perspective. Yan Mingfu was no apologist for the things Mao did wrong. But he perhaps put them in their fuller context: that Mao, above all, was struggling to unify a country that had torn itself apart for decades, and because of its internal weaknesses it had been abused and exploited by the imperial powers of Britain, Russia, Japan, France and America for a long time. Mao ended that exploitation. He introduced one language to a polyglot people, he drew everything under the control of one government, he united a fractured country, he promoted equal rights for women, he banned abortion–

'What about the Cultural Revolution?' interjected Fraser, a little slyly.

'Ah,' sighed Yan Mingfu, 'yes. Well, as a student of history, you will have heard of Madame Jiang.'

'Mao's wife.'

'His fourth one, yes. If anyone was responsible for the Cultural Revolution, it was she,' he continued, describing how Madame Jiang had begun her career as an actress during the heady days of the 1920s in Imperial Shanghai. But, as an actress, she was hopeless. Devoid of talent, and rejected time and again by the artistic and theatrical elites of the day, her career floundered, leaving her enraged and embittered. Later, as Mao's wife, she saw an opportunity to exact her revenge. The notorious Red Guards of the Cultural Revolution were her invention, Yan Mingfu told us. 'And where did they begin?' He smiled. 'In Shanghai, rounding up the theatre directors, the authors, the academics, journalists, decadent actors, musicians, artists and so on; anyone successful in the arts. The theatres were smashed, the libraries burned, the universities destroyed . . . all because of a woman scorned, as you say.'

'But if Mao didn't really support this, then why did he let her do it?'

'She had a hold over him. Mao had certain . . . weaknesses, of which she was only too aware.'

'What kind of weaknesses?' I asked, perhaps showing my naïvety.

Yan Mingfu said nothing for a few moments, and then, 'You have to understand that China has always been ruled by emperors . . . Those emperors have always had their concubines.' An indulgent smile played over his lips. 'Chairman Mao, also, was an emperor of China.'

Like I said, it was an extraordinary evening.

The following day, I received a phone call from Mr Shí. 'We would like to invite you to join the delegation travelling to London in two weeks' time for the Special Olympics bid,' he said.

'Me?' I was honoured, but somewhat surprised. 'What do you think I can bring to the bid?'

He simply replied, 'Your presence has been requested.'

As you may remember, my own connection with Shanghai had

begun with those two tickets to the 'Special Olympics Opening Ceremony' way back in 1996. Then, there had been some confusion about exactly what event it was we were watching; this time, it was the real deal. And, naturally, I was delighted to be involved on our adoptive city's behalf.

Even so, as the only foreigner on a delegation full of extremely senior civic and party officials, I did want to stay on side with my friends in the British government. I contacted the Foreign Office and let them know what was happening. In fact, they were incredibly supportive of the situation and gave me the number of the British ambassador to China, who would also be in London for the event, and told me to call him if there was anything I needed from them.

It was early July 2002 and a beautiful time to be in London, with the parks and avenues in their full flush of green foliage, and the air alive with that buzz that comes from the English enjoying the summer sun.

Among the group were several government ministers, of whom Yan Mingfu was one. The delegation was headed up by Deng Pufang, the son of Deng Xiaoping, the reformist leader of the People's Republic of China who had succeeded Chairman Mao.

Deng Pufang was considered a natural choice to lead Shanghai's bid for the Special Olympics because he himself was a paraplegic, as well being head of the People's Disability Federation. During the early years of the Cultural Revolution, Mao's Red Guards had seized him and thrown him out of a third-floor window at Beijing University. He was rushed to hospital but was refused admission because he was the son of a known capitalist. By the time he reached another clinic, the damage was done. His back was broken and he was left paralysed. By the time of this delegation, he was in his late fifties.

No expense was spared. We all stayed in the Hilton Hotel on Hyde Park Corner, and for the first few days it was all about the bid. The field had been whittled down to a straightforward contest between New York City and Shanghai. When Shanghai won, I

wish I could have said my presence had in some way contributed
to the eventual result but, in truth, I had been feeling at a bit of
a loose end. Even so, I was as delighted as anyone that Shanghai
had won, and in true Chinese style it was decided that we should
have a big party in a Chinese restaurant in Canary Wharf to
celebrate the victory.

At last I was given something useful to do. Deng Pufang and
his wheelchair weren't able to get on the bus transporting the
delegates down to Canary Wharf, so they asked me to drive him
to the restaurant. I was only too glad to. They had hired a special
car – a Mercedes, I think – that could accommodate his chair in
the back, so we all got in.

Everything was fine, we were ready to go, the bus started to
pull away and I was to follow. It was only as I reached to release
the handbrake that I realised it wasn't there. I had no idea they
had changed the design of handbrakes like that, and for the life
of me I could not find any other switch or button that looked
likely to serve that function. The bus was turning into the busy
traffic on Park Lane and I was starting to sweat. I couldn't afford
to get left behind because I had no idea where the restaurant was
or even how to get to Canary Wharf, and to make Deng Pufang
late for the party because I was lost, driving around in circles in
the East End, would have caused him serious loss of face.

I came to a rather frantic decision and drove off with the
handbrake still firmly on, warning lights flashing, alert beeping
angrily. Very quickly the car started to be filled with the stink of
melting brake pads. Realising something was wrong, my passen-
gers in the back seemed to think it was highly amusing, and they
wound down the windows and laughed away while I gritted my
teeth around the Hyde Park Corner traffic system and headed off
down Constitution Hill towards Buckingham Palace.

We were some distance down The Mall, a good half a mile
further on, before I finally noticed a button with a 'P' on it. I
pressed it, and the Mercedes gave a violent lurch as it careened
forward down the road, nearly ramming the car in front. I was

deeply, deeply embarrassed, but Deng Pufang and the others in the back only laughed all the harder. And when we did arrive safely at the restaurant in convoy with the bus, they took great pleasure in recounting the story to the other delegates, who all found the incident hilarious. I was christened 'Handbrake Bob' on the spot. I think the first *gan bei* (a toast offered by the Chinese at meals for social and business purposes) of the party was a toast to my woeful driving.

Later that evening, I was approached by Yan Mingfu. He asked whether I would like to join him and his wife for dinner the following evening. They had a table booked at a little French place around the corner from the Hilton. I said I would be honoured to.

So the next evening, I found myself seated opposite Yan Mingfu and his wife in the intimate surroundings of a small bistro-style restaurant in Shepherd Market. His wife's English was impeccable. His was good, but whenever he felt the need to express himself more fully he would switch to Mandarin and she would translate.

'Do you know why you are here?' he began. 'On the delegation, I mean?'

I shuffled on my seat. 'My love for Shanghai?' I suggested. It sounded a bit lame.

'Hmm,' he said, with an elusive smile. 'It was not to drive cars, anyway.' He paused and took a slow sip of his beloved Bordeaux. 'Robert, I should like to tell you about my father.'

I knew something of his past already, of course, from our previous conversations and things people had told me. But I knew nothing of what he was about to reveal.

'My father was a pastor in Shenyang,' he said, his voice growing softer, almost reverent. 'A man of God, like you. He went on to become head of the YMCA in China. And then, in 1927, the British YMCA funded him to go to university in Edinburgh.' He described what his father had passed on to him of his time in Europe: his studies in Edinburgh and some travel to London and then to Paris. These memories were clearly precious to his son.

Yan Mingfu smiled as he recalled them. Then a darker expression fell across his face. 'As an old man, he was imprisoned during the Cultural Revolution. So was I. Both of us were put in solitary confinement for two years.' He paused. Another sip. 'When I came out, I couldn't speak, and I found my father dying.'

He explained how, during the Cultural Revolution, the Red Guards had destroyed everything, all traces of those who fell foul of their narrow ideology. There were no photos left of his father now, no memorabilia.

He looked me in the eye. 'Is it possible that you could take me up to Edinburgh to the university? I want to see if there is any record of him in their archives.'

I was hanging off every word, of course, and at once I thought of the telephone number the Foreign Office had given me to call if ever I needed assistance.

'I think I can help,' I said. 'Leave it with me.'

After the dinner, I called the number. The ambassador picked up immediately.

'Can it be done?' I asked, after I had explained what it was that Yan Mingfu wanted.

'Absolutely,' he replied.

'But on a Sunday? There'll be no one there.'

'We'll sort that. Don't worry. Just get him a train ticket to Edinburgh. We'll do the rest.'

So we travelled up there on the Sunday, and there was the dean of the university to meet us off the train. He showed us around, and in due course he took us down into the archives where they had found photographs of Yan Mingfu's father in Edinburgh, another in Trafalgar Square and one beside the Eiffel Tower in Paris. His father peered out from these old sepia images, a tall, elegant man in a suit and tie, wearing round glasses. Seeing them, these fading shadows of his past, Yan Mingfu broke down and wept.

The delegation returned to China two days later. Almost immediately I received word that Yan Mingfu had fallen sick – quite seriously sick – and that he was being cared for in one of the top hospitals in Beijing, the special preserve of only the top party officials in the capital. I took a trip up there to visit him on his sickbed, not knowing whether I should be worried that I was about to lose my guardian angel.

I visited him twice. The first time there was an American present, but the second time there were only other Chinese present, and I felt he would not need to maintain any kind of pretence in front of his subordinate countrymen. I asked him whether I could pray for him. He nodded, holding his hands out over the coverlet to receive prayer, in the same way you would expect anyone familiar with the ways of the church to do.

So I prayed for him. Nothing grand. A few simple words. Afterwards, I said, 'Mr Yan, you may not want to answer this, but I have to ask you . . . are you a Christian?'

I watched his chest rise and fall a couple of times before he answered. 'President Bush,' he said, 'wears his Christianity on his arm. Others have to guard theirs very closely in their heart.'

I smiled, because now I had my answer. And I could only marvel at how God had woven all this together.

16: Riding the Dragon's Back

I've breathed the mountain air, man
Of travel I've a-had my share, man
I've been everywhere.
(Johnny Cash)*

Yan Mingfu recovered from his illness. Soon after, he told me that we should move to Beijing.

It made sense. My contract with the Shanghai Civil Affairs Bureau had come to a successful conclusion in September 2001. Since then, I had been 'out of contract' – at least with respect to the Chinese government – even though Care for Children had continued to work hard with the three other projects in the meantime. But it was time for the next wave of expansion, and if it was going to come from the top down, then Beijing was where we needed to be.

We moved there in the middle of 2003.

It was hard. There was no doubt about that. As a family, we had invested a lot of ourselves into building a strong life in Shanghai. Each one of us had friends that we would leave behind. We knew the city, we had got used to the climate and we understood the people (well, we thought we did). So for all of us, Beijing was a strange and unknown beast.

For a start, as a city it's a lot larger, sprawled over a huge urbanised area. The traffic is appalling, and although the pollution

* Johnny Cash, 'I've been everywhere' (1996).

when we first moved there was nothing like as bad as it would soon become with all the construction for the 2008 Summer Olympics, I quickly had to accept that doing anything in the city would take a lot longer than it had in Shanghai. The distances between the places I needed to be were so far and the traffic so dense that often it would take most of a working day just to drive across town, have a meeting and return to the office. I had to make peace with the fact that the pace of life was going to be slower.

We were fortunate to arrive in the summertime. The city was hot and dusty and a lot drier than the soggy swelter of a Shanghai summer, but the winters in Beijing were truly brutal. The mercury could drop towards minus ten, even minus twenty sometimes. And the air was dry, so dry. There was almost no precipitation from late November through to late April. My hands would split with a thousand tiny cracks because of the lack of moisture in the air. Any sign of life receded completely – the trees were stripped back to miserable skeletons of their summer selves, and any whisper of grass or plant life in the parks and public spaces withered far underground. And as it was so cold, all human life had to retreat inside, too, as families and individuals bunkered down in their apartments for the long, dark months. We were forever piling on or stripping off clothing to come in from or go out into the cold.

The people of Beijing were very different, too. The Shanghainese are fast talkers, wheeler-dealers, entrepreneurs and more than a little sly. I found the Beijingers a lot more direct and honest to deal with. The pace of life was slower. It had to be because everything happened at glacial speed. This was the seat of power, the heart of government, of the arts, of education, of the old culture of China. Shanghai was all about high finance and big business, about making a buck. If you were to leave your wallet in the back of a taxi in Beijing, the driver would drive miles to return it to you. That would never happen in Shanghai.

Once we started to settle in, we liked it. There was always

another little neighbourhood to explore, each one almost a village within a city, with its own distinctive style and atmosphere. Little artisanal streets decked out with red paper lanterns; sketchers and painters in the parks and musicians on street corners. Cyclists everywhere. Wet markets, dry markets. We found authentic canteens hidden away down back alleys where, seated at crooked little wooden tables on wobbly stools, you could eat the most delicious Beijing duck for a couple of yuan, or Mongolian hotpot that steamed in your face and burned your throat, or any number of the dishes that distinguished Beijing cuisine from what we had known in Shanghai.

At the weekends, there was far more for a family to do outside Beijing than there had been outside Shanghai. The Great Wall was a short drive away. There were mountains to hike, lakes to swim in. And when spring did come . . . boy, it came quickly. First the rain, then the temperature shot up from below freezing to sixteen or seventeen degrees in a few days. From one week to the next, the city exploded with life; pink and white blossom floated on the air; the people unfurled into the public spaces like the leaves on the trees, filling the city squares and parks with music and games and dancing. It was beautiful. And, aside from the natural rhythms of the year, Beijing was a city on the ascendant. Indeed, as the following years would prove, it was rising like a comet.

Care for Children had a beautiful new office in Silver Tower in west central Beijing. On a clear day, you could see the Great Wall on the blue hills far beyond the city limits. We had four or five people on the team by now, having brought a small but select crew with us from Shanghai: myself, Sunny, and Thomas Abbott – a young Englishman who had arrived in Shanghai in 2000 to teach English language and who had since come to work for me. In those short years he had become a dear friend of the Glover family. In fact, it wouldn't be long before he would become a permanent member of it, as his friendship with our eldest daughter, Rachel, blossomed into love and, later, marriage. Our driver, Kong Ming, had also stuck with us, having driven the red minibus that the British Chamber of Commerce had donated to our family the twelve hundred kilometres north to Beijing, together with the herd of stray cats we had adopted. We also still had Priscilla, our lead training manager.

That was more or less it on the Care for Children side. We had managed to keep our overheads incredibly low. Besides this team in China, there was John Langlois back on Guernsey, who took care of Care for Children's administrative and legal responsibilities as a UK-registered charity; and we were supported by our astonishingly able board members, consisting of Lord Laming as chairman, John Langlois of course, Sir David Brewer, Sir John Chalstrey, Fraser White, James McIlwraith, Lady Tessa Keswick and Richard Graham. All the fundraising and operational side of the organisation was run out of China.

Thanks to the unseen but ever-present hand of Yan Mingfu, the Chinese government already had a very clear strategy when we arrived. The plan was to roll out the same family placement project that had proven so successful in Shanghai to another fifteen provinces.

The way it was structured was in a kind of three-way partnership. At the top was the Ministry of Civil Affairs. This was a central government authority who issued the decree that effectively made that roll-out strategy the law of the land. Thus, we had the full weight of the governmental apparatus behind us. The Ministry of Civil Affairs then delegated the implementation of that strategy to the China Social Work Association (CSWA). This was what they call a government–non-government organisation, or GANGO (a contradiction in terms anywhere but in China). Essentially it was an NGO that was run by a government official, usually a recently retired minister or vice minister. The ex-minister in charge of the CSWA was a man called Xu Rui Xing. He had been a subordinate of Yan Mingfu when Mr Yan had been Minister of Civil Affairs. In other words, while he was a considerable force to be reckoned with in his own right within the party hierarchy, he did what Yan Mingfu wanted him to. That meant working with us.

Care for Children had an initial three-year partnership contract with the CSWA. We were going to roll out family placement programmes in the following places: Ürümqi in the far western province of Xinjiang; Hengfeng and Yifeng in Jiangxi province; Yuncheng, Datong and Yan'an in Shanxi province; Guiyang in Guizhou province; Bengbu in Anhui province; Jingdong in Yunnan province; Wuhan in Hubei province; Xining in Qinghai province; Yinchuan in Ningxia province (with whom we had already been talking); Chengdu in Sichuan (where the Lamberts were already at work); Lanzhou in Gansu province; and Baotou in Inner Mongolia.

I imagine most, if not all, of these names will be meaningless to most readers, barely pronounceable names of cities you are never likely to have cause to visit. But if you were to look at a map of the provinces of China, you would soon see the swathes of that vast nation that this list encompasses (not to mention the millions of people each city represents): almost every province in the west, except for Tibet, and several in central, southern and eastern China.

The plan for this first wave of expansion was ambitious, to say the least. But thanks to Yan Mingfu, we had the means to achieve it. And wherever we went, almost without exception, we had the full weight of the central government's authority behind us. That meant open doors and green lights. The dragon had spread its wings, and it was time to climb on its back.

Over the next three years, I travelled the length and breadth of China by air, rail and road. From Xining with its thin air and crystal-bright skies perched on the rim of the Tibetan plateau to the black shale wastelands of the Gobi Desert in the north; from far-off Ürümqi nestled in the foothills of the Heavenly Mountains to the soggy river-lands of Anhui in the east. I saw it all. A whirlwind of travel that was exhausting and exhilarating in equal measure.

I travelled with Care for Children local staff, and wherever we went, the attention was relentless from the moment we stepped off the plane or train. This was a cultural thing. In each city, I was the responsibility of the local civil authorities, and, as a friend of Yan Mingfu and with the standing orders of the central government to get this project done, no expense was spared. I was their charge from the second I arrived to the second they put me back on the train or plane, and there was barely a minute of respite in between.

Often we would be greeted by a military guard and taken straight off to meet the mayor or some other local worthy. Then there were dinners, cultural excursions to places of local interest, more banqueting, visits to the orphanages in question and drives out into the countryside to visit potential placement communities or other smaller care facilities. These could be two or three hours' drive away, and we would often stop for a huge lunch in some select restaurant along the way, then drive back to the city for more ceremony, more food, more *baijiu*. There was a great deal of bravado; many of the local officials directing the orphanages were former (or even current) military men, and they made much of my days in the Royal Navy.

For the most part, we found a huge appetite to receive what we had to offer. The only downside was that, without a minute to myself for days at a time, I would often return to Liz in Beijing a husk of the man who had left her.

But it was worth it.

This was all good *guangxi*. We were building a network of connections, a community of purpose that was going to transform the nature of orphan care across the entire nation. In order to cultivate that sense of common purpose, we organised regional training workshops, which took place perhaps every other month, and staff would travel for days and over huge distances in order to attend. If we held one in, say, Chengdu, people would come all the way from Ürümqi in the west, or from Yunnan and Guizhou in the south. A small handful of us could be training hundreds of orphanage staff at a time.

Besides the site visits and regional workshops, we would hold a National Childcare Conference every two years, either in Beijing or Shanghai, to which we would invite everyone, from the very top down. Lord Laming, one of Care for Children's board members, gave the keynote speech on a number of occasions. On the Chinese side, we would invite the incumbent Minister of Civil Affairs. Mr Shí would come, and Yan Mingfu. In addition, all the top government officials were involved, like Xu Rui Xing, the head of CSWA, along with all the regional orphanage directors and their teams.

On the first day we would have the big speeches and presentations from outside experts or the senior figures. The next day, each region would have an opportunity to present to the conference about how its project was going, illustrated with statistics and stories and things they had learned (usually from experience). We also had a big exhibition hall where each province set up a stand so that the VIPs could circulate and discuss each project face to face with those on the ground. It became an extraordinarily creative event. Not only was it a great exchange of best practice ideas, each province learning from the others' experiences, but there was a healthy competitive element to it as well (especially after we started giving awards for 'best in class'). The more junior provincial officials wanted to shine in front of their superiors, gaining 'face'. And with the Shanghai project providing the model that it *could* be done well, none of the other provinces wanted to be the one lagging behind.

It was also fascinating to see how different provinces developed different areas of expertise. For example, the project in Yinchuan became specialist in developing equipment for disabled children. The project in Chengdu created a very advanced programme of community education, bringing together the children and families from different towns and villages to learn and progress together. The Beijing team became expert in monitoring statistics. This was unity in diversity in action. And, of course, the great thing was that everyone came back the following year to report on their progress, having implemented each other's best practices.

It was the most effective motor for change I've ever witnessed.

At the end of each conference, we would have a big party, to which each team would come dressed in costumes traditional to their province. We soon struck upon the idea that each province should put on some sort of performance for the rest. So one minute you might have the staff from Inner Mongolia dressed head to toe like Genghis Khan, singing in rich, resonant baritone voices about the harsh wind blowing across the empty grasslands of the steppe; the next you'd have the team from Yunnan, under tall headdresses tinkling with bells, trilling away in their high, nasal pitch about peach blossom and the misty peaks of the south. It was quite wonderful to see it all coming together.

As if things could get any more bizarre, one day in 2005 I had a phone call from Sir Christopher Hun, the British ambassador in Beijing. He informed me that the Queen was going to honour me with an Order of the British Empire (OBE). I nearly dropped the phone, and it took me a while to reply with anything coherent.

'You are going to accept it, aren't you?' asked Christopher, worried that my silence was a sign of my lack of interest.

'Yes, I'm just surprised!' I replied.

When I called my mother, she was bursting with pride. I was able to take three people with me to the ceremony at Buckingham Palace. So I took Liz, Anna, who was studying at Dean Close in Cheltenham at the time and came in her school uniform, and Mum. I wore a Chinese suit with a high-neck collar for the occasion. I was pleased with my outfit, until two old ladies walked passed me in the hotel lobby and said, 'Morning, Father,' thinking I was a priest!

My mother was frail and had to be in a wheelchair, but she had her own personal butler for the day, who gallantly wheeled her around.

I was humbled when I saw the other people who were being honoured with me, one of whom was Lance Corporal Johnson Beharry. He was awarded the Victoria Cross, which is the highest military decoration for valour in the British and Commonwealth armed forces, for twice saving members of his unit from ambushes in Iraq. Ellen MacArthur, who in February 2005 broke the world record for the fastest solo circumnavigation of the globe, was also given an OBE.

So where was God in all this? Well, everywhere. All of this was covered in prayer. But we were given a special insight into how deep his influence went the first time I went to Baotou, the provincial capital of Inner Mongolia. I was travelling with Shi Guoshan, the government official representing the CSWA, who often accompanied me on these trips.

It was an overnight rail journey heading west, on a train packed with people passing the time smoking and playing cards. Not exactly conducive to a great night's sleep. At a certain point, Shi Guoshan started talking about the kinds of people we would be meeting. 'I know you are a Christian,' he smiled sympathetically, 'but I'm afraid you will find no Christians in Baotou.'

'That's fine,' I replied. 'We're here to place orphans in families, whatever they or the families believe.'

In some ways, our reception in Baotou was typical. We were met off the train by an army escort and driven straight to a lunch with the mayor. What wasn't typical was how rough I felt and looked, after a very poor night's sleep in our smoke-filled compartment. I needed a wash, a shave, a change of clothes and some decent fresh air. Instead we were whisked off to the People's Hall of Baotou with a police escort, all sirens blaring. The Mayor of Baotou was waiting for us, immaculately groomed in a slick suit. I looked quite the opposite, in jeans and an old jumper and with hair sticking out at all angles.

Introductions were made and we were ushered into the hall, where there was a large dining table. I was seated next to the mayor with two translators sitting close behind, and Shi Guoshan was seated on the other side of the mayor. It turned out that this was the official opening ceremony of the placement project and they had organised for twenty sets of parents who would be receiving orphans to be present.

At a certain point in the ceremony, it was Shi Guoshan's moment to introduce me to the assembly. He stood and, as he introduced me, he made some joke about my being English and also a Christian. I didn't quite catch the meaning, but he clearly intended it to be funny. However, none of the families laughed. Instead there was an awkward silence, so Shi Guoshan, obviously feeling uncomfortable, repeated what he had said. Again, a pregnant silence. Then one of the parents, an older woman, put up her hand and declared that she too, in fact, was a Christian. And one by one, every single one of the twenty couples raised their hands to indicate that they, too, were Christians.

It was astonishing – to me, as much as to anyone else – that every single one of them was a Christian. And certainly it was clear that Shi Guoshan felt embarrassed by the incident. On the journey home, he brought it up. 'I had no idea that there were Christians in Inner Mongolia,' he said. 'Tell me, *why* are they helping these children?'

Seeing that his question was sincerely meant, I told him that it was part of the teaching in the New Testament, that Christians are called upon to care for orphans; that it's the duty of all Christians to act like Jesus and to put others' needs before their own. He was taken aback. It seemed to have never occurred to him that Christians could be anything other than, at best, problematic for the government, or at worst, a collection of troublemakers.

When we got back to Beijing, he contacted three of the other projects in order to find out the religions of the families who had taken on orphans. He discovered that 80 per cent of them were Christian.

The figure was as surprising to me as it was to him. Although

I am a Christian and willing to share the gospel with anyone in my personal life, Care for Children was not and is not a Christian organisation. We didn't proselytise the children, the families or the staff. As far as I was concerned, God had given me this little piece of the jigsaw to take care of, to do what I had been called to do. That took obedience and faith, to trust that it was God who would complete the jigsaw. But the fact that such a substantial proportion of the families who came forward to offer love and security to those orphans were Christians told me that God was working at a depth and breadth far beyond anything I could comprehend. It was the first real glimpse of the bigger picture: that God was working to transform this nation, and that our work was just a small part of his larger plan.

This was the first time that the central government had taken on board that Christians were, in a civic sense, model citizens who could help them bring about beneficial change to China.

Of course, the party's attitude to the Church in general changed with any change in leadership at the very top. Until 2005, the Premier was Jiang Zemin, who later went on record to say that he would have liked to have made China a Christian nation, which stunned a lot of people.

Jiang was succeeded by Hu Jintao, a Buddhist. President Hu's great emphasis was on creating a 'harmonious society' throughout China. What that meant in practice was a time of leniency for Christians, and, interestingly, the growth of the Church slowed during that period. Under Xi Jinping, on the other hand, who is in many ways a reversion to the old Maoist style of government and therefore a lot harder on the Church, Christianity has flourished.

The inescapable lesson seems to be that the more pressure you apply to the Church, the faster it grows. Persecution leads to revival. The inversion of that rule is also true, and something we in the West would do well to note: where religious tolerance increases, so too does spiritual lethargy. To create holy fire, you need heat.

It is worth noting that in China, where religious persecution has been prevalent for several decades, even official figures estimate that the Church has now grown to around sixty million souls. The true figure, I believe, is double that.

You might wonder where the obstacles were in all of this. Everything seemed to be moving in one direction – the right direction. And the truth is, the demand to implement the family placement programme around the country was so high that we didn't have the time or the capacity to hang around for those who didn't want it. Where things got held up in one place, we simply moved forward in another.

Lanzhou, for example, never really took off, and the tone for that was set from the start. On our first visit there, again I was with Shi Guoshan. We were shown into the office of the director of the Lanzhou orphanage and it was like stepping back in time twenty years. There was a big photograph of Mao on the director's desk, and a huge hammer and sickle banner draped across the wall behind him. I launched into my patter about the benefits of family care over institutional care and what we could do for his orphans, how we would work alongside his staff in support of them, and so on. He listened, stony-faced, puffing his way through half a pack of cigarettes while I talked. He was ex-military, a party man of the old school who, so I had heard, had fallen out of favour and been assigned to running the orphanage as a punishment for whatever had been his misdemeanour.

'And we can run this project in the community for the same price as your electricity bill,' I said, coming to the end of my pitch.

Silence.

I knew his orphanage was in crisis, as so many across China were, thanks to the enormous numbers of abandoned children who were the unintended consequences of the one-child policy. The figures for his institution were something like eight hundred children being housed in a facility designed for three hundred.

'How many children do you want to place during the first project?' I asked, trying to provoke a response.

The old fellow thought about it, taking another deep drag on his cigarette, then expelling plumes of yellow smoke across the desk. '*Wushí.*' Fifty.

'Fine. Then I'll need to train three of your staff as family placement workers,' I replied. I had to explain to him that, to begin with, the orphanage's costs would increase slightly. But Care for Children would offset this increase by paying 50 per cent of the fostering allowances as well as the training costs. In three to five years, the budget increase would start to reverse, and would then drop below its pre-project levels. At that point we would hand the project over to the orphanage to run it themselves.

Part of the problem was a basic limitation of thinking about how best to care for orphans. Before my arrival in China, the system of care stood upon three pillars of value: Health, Education, Living. This was a party slogan, and we saw those words everywhere. Each staff member was classified within one of those three silos. They were either a medic, a teacher or someone to impart to the children basic life skills. There was nothing about the emotional support of each child, nothing to address their social needs, and nothing to address the many cases of the physical needs of those suffering from a disability. So when we came, speaking about those things, it was breaking new ground. We had to radically expand their thinking beyond the narrow confines of those three values. In some places this was harder than in others. And I could see in Lanzhou, just from walking around the place, that each staff member was an official, and nothing more.

Besides reshaping their thinking, we often had to allay initial fears that we were coming in to do them out of a job. If all the orphans were placed outside the orphanage, what function would it serve? It would be obsolete, wouldn't it? So, then, what would all the staff do? But that wasn't what we intended. Our aim was to bring the institution *into* the community so that, in the end, a director such as this man would be running a professional service centre of educational trainers, family placement workers, physiotherapists and psychologists, as well as continuing to run a small residential care home for children not yet placed with families. Ultimately this would alleviate the over-crowding crisis, reduce their overhead costs and, most importantly, it would be better for the children.

My explanation of all this to the Lanzhou director was again met with silence.

'So what do you think?' I said, feeling ever more frustrated at the stonewall treatment.

He leaned forward, propped his elbows on the desk and stee-pled his fingers. 'Can you give me ten million yuan to build a new orphanage?' he croaked. That was roughly US$1.5 million. But the money wasn't the point. The message had fallen on completely deaf ears.

'Robert,' interjected Shi Guoshan, 'would you mind leaving the room for a minute?'

I stepped outside into the corridor. The door closed. I then listened – it was hard not to – while Shi Guoshan gave the director full vent of his feelings. A few minutes of yelling later, I was invited back into the room. Shi Guoshan informed me that the director had agreed to start the project.

Unsurprisingly, our work did not go well in Lanzhou. It was one of the least successful projects in all of China.

Where the projects did work, the results were always remark-able to behold. On one trip, I took Lord Laming up to the high-altitude city of Xining in Qinghai province. He and his wife accompanied me on a visit to a village where several severely disabled orphans had been placed. There we found families with very little, living in small clay-brick houses with newspapers pasted to the walls for insulation against the cold. Strings of chillies and garlic hung outside, the dry air preserving them perfectly, and in each house was a *kang*, a large bedding area for the whole family, built over a coal-fire stove to keep them warm through the freezing winters. Despite their simple living, Lord Laming commented, 'You could search the length and breadth of

England and never find families that would take children like this and love them in the way these Chinese mothers do.'

He may have been right.

Even so, that community *was* extremely poor. And while I had always maintained that a child would always be better off being raised in a loving family environment – however poor – than in even the best-quality residential care home, I was about to have my convictions tested.

When I went to Guiyang, the city in the south-west of Guizhou province, I found a brand-new orphanage awaiting me. This was towards the end of our first three-year contract with the CSWA, which ran to 2006. In 2005, Jiang Zemin had been succeeded by Hu Jintao, and this change in leadership naturally had a knock-on effect down the party hierarchy. We had seen a change of personnel at the very top of the Ministry of Civil Affairs, and while that didn't bring an end to our activities, it did mean that our work would now run alongside several other initiatives the government wanted to introduce in the area of social welfare. One of these was a programme of reinvestment in the orphanage facilities around the country. The one in Guiyang was one of the first to be completed.

The results were spectacular. Everything about it was of the highest calibre, especially the director, an inspirational young woman in her late twenties who was running her orphanage with great love and care. She told me that, although the families living in the nearby communities were poor, they had already placed some children with them. As we walked around her brand-new building, the place was filled with the sound of children playing. The rooms were bright and cheerful, the teaching facilities and playgrounds were impressive, the washrooms and dormitories all pristine.

The more I saw, the more a gloom began to settle over me, not because I didn't want the children in residential care to be well looked after, but because even I started to wonder whether a child would actually be better off in a facility like this than placed in a family that was living in very basic conditions. And I knew if that thought had occurred to me, it was more than likely to occur to those in positions of oversight in the Chinese government. Suddenly, I felt the wind draining from the sails of our work. Was it all going to be superseded by these flash new buildings, brightly coloured swings and slides, and squeaky-clean floors?

But that afternoon, we were taken to visit a nearby village where they had placed some of the children. It was quite the off-road experience to reach it. We drove for about ten miles up a muddy mountain road, lurching about like a drunken bronco, till I felt quite sick. When, at last, we reached the village, I got out of the vehicle, desperate for some fresh air. I was immediately accosted by a small boy with a long bamboo stick. He was about six years old and his name was Xiao Ming. His clothes were nothing but a scruffy red tracksuit top, a ragged pair of shorts and blue shoes. He seemed to be furious, his little face turning puce with anger, but I couldn't for the life of me think why. I dodged his blows, caught hold of the stick and tugged it from his hand. He then proceeded to yell at me at the top of his voice. It was only later that someone came to my rescue and translated what he was saying.

'See that tree,' he had cried, pointing across the field. 'I climbed that tree yesterday and I got to the top of that tree.' He clenched his little fists tighter. 'Everyone in the village came to see me in that tree and they called my name to come down. Everyone here knows my name.' He then pointed to a nearby building. 'See that place. That is my school. I go there every day. And this – this is my dog!' he shouted at the top of his voice, pointing to a brown mongrel lurking nearby. 'Every day I go to school and my dog follows me, and when I finish he is waiting for me at the gates and we walk home together. In the village we pass my auntie's fruit shop. She knows my name and gives me an apple. My other auntie there,' he pointed to another shop front, 'she gives me broken biscuits and she knows my name, too. I have a mother and father and brothers and sisters now. And I will *not* go back to the orphanage with you!'

When this was explained to me, I realised that this little boy had seen the orphanage minibus arrive in his remote village and assumed that it had come to take him back there. I was speechless. What he had just yelled in his infantile outrage was a far more authentic picture of his community than I ever could have articulated. Here he had a family, adults looking out for him, games he liked to play, a school, even his own dog!

Xiao Ming's words showed me that the issue was not material possessions or giving the children a certain standard of living. It was about giving them a sense of identity, security and belonging. Here, this little boy was known and loved as an individual, not merely one of hundreds of other orphans. Xiao Ming's family may have been poor, but he was free to do things he never could have done in an orphanage, like climbs trees and keep a dog of his own.

My doubts were answered in a stroke.

The Guiyang project was exceptional in another way. A few months later, I was in the United States at a conference when I was approached by a man who invited me to have breakfast with him the following day. When we met, he told me he was a pastor who had been supporting the house churches in Guizhou province. For a while they had been growing at a rapid pace, but then, a few years earlier, that pace had begun to slow. The church had seemed to dip into a decline. He likened it to a story in the book of Acts, when certain disciples had received the Holy Spirit but had not gone out to share the good news or to serve the community. Instead they stayed and preached only in Jerusalem, and did not scatter more widely until after the stoning of Stephen. Similarly, he told me, the Christians in Guizhou had remained inward-looking and had been reluctant to serve their community. The result was, spiritually, for them, a very dry and unfruitful time.

'But then,' said the pastor, 'couples responded to the orphanage's appeal for families to take on orphans. They started taking in children from your project, and when they did, revival started to break out.' His face was glowing as he described how the community saw the Christians' faith in action at last. 'They had been watching them and now they saw something attractive, they wanted to know more.' He said since then they had never seen such rapid growth in the house churches.

This story drove home the message to me again, loud and clear. As long as we were obedient to what God had asked us to do, he would do the rest.

17: Joe

___

God wants us to have soft hearts and hard feet.
The trouble with so many of us is that
we have hard hearts and soft feet.
(Jackie Pullinger)

As a family, we had two goals in China. One was to place orphans with families. The other was to love the poor as Jesus would.

Naturally, I took the lead on the first of those. But over our years in Guernsey and then in China, I had watched Liz take the most remarkable lead in loving the poor. There was no length to which she wouldn't go to help someone impoverished and in need of comfort on the street. Food, clothing, shelter: she shared it all, and her influence on me and our children was profound.

In Shanghai, after leaving our huge house in Beverley Hills, for a time we lived in quite a smart residential apartment block called Mandarin Gardens, before we downsized even further to a little three-bedroom apartment on Hong Mei Lu.

Mandarin Gardens was the kind of residential compound that had security guards at the gate. I'm not sure they ever got used to Liz coming and going with the old lady with a cloth on her head. (Not so much 'lady in the van' as 'lady with the rag'.) She became quite the regular house guest at Mandarin Gardens – she would stay for a shower, a piece of Liz's homemade cake and then a snooze on our sofa while Liz washed her clothes.

Most people reckoned the old lady was mad; she could often be seen standing on the side of the nearby eight-lane highway with a wet cloth on her head, waving a stick angrily at the sky. At whom or what for, no one knew. She was eccentric, to say the least. But Liz and she became firm friends. And the old lady seemed to enjoy nothing more than sitting on our sofa eating Liz's cake. After her nap, she would hobble off on her way.

This sort of thing – inviting homeless people in to enjoy a few basic comforts before sending them out again – became so habitual in our house that our children started to emulate the behaviour that Liz modelled so well. Our third daughter, Megan, had a boyfriend during that time who was the son of the Ecuadorian ambassador. There was one occasion – now legend in Glover family lore – when the ambassador's wife came home to find a homeless man in her kitchen, with Megan loading him up with food from her fridge. Needless to say, she hit the roof.

While we were still in Shanghai, Jackie Pullinger came to live with us for a period. By then, I had known her for five years. After the instant connection of our first meeting, I had been a regular visitor to her ministry in Hong Kong, as I had promised. As it grew, our friendship felt more like a blood brother–sister relationship. We developed a deep understanding of one another and looked out for each other when things got difficult.

Around the turn of the millennium and for a while after, Jackie went through a tough time. Her husband, John, had passed away and she was experiencing deep grief and loss over that. She needed a rest from her ministry, which was understandable given how demanding it was.

We invited her to Shanghai to live with us on a kind of furlough, and she stayed for several months. I hope we were able to give her the love and support she needed. What I do know, though, is what she gave us. Her passion for the poor was irrepressible. And completely boundless, it seemed. She had a famous saying, which became widely known throughout the Church: 'God wants us to have soft hearts and hard feet. The trouble with so many of us is that we have hard hearts and soft feet.'

I remember other things she would tell us, such as, 'I went up to a man and said, "Jesus loves you," but I realised that it didn't mean anything unless I did it.' Or, 'It's very much easier to do what God made you for, than not.' It was such a blessing to have that time with her. And I know Jackie had a profound influence on Liz, who took her words to heart.

So when we moved to Beijing, Liz wasted no time before she was seeking out the poor and turning the love of Christ into action. One woman Liz met had to beg on the streets in order to send money home to her children, who lived in a different province with her parents. She had her baby daughter with her who was only eighteen months old. Liz and our daughter Anna were out shopping when they came across the pair, and so Liz asked the woman in halting Chinese whether they would like to come home with them for a bath and a meal. The woman agreed and followed Liz and Anna back to the car. On the drive home, the woman said her name was Gaojie and her baby was called Lu Lu.

Once back at the house, Liz ran a bath for them and then went downstairs to cook something for them to eat. When she went back, she found Gaojie still in the bath, breastfeeding her baby, and Anna was in there with them, washing the baby's back with a soap and flannel. For a fleeting second, Liz panicked, concerned that Anna might catch the skin condition from which the mother was clearly suffering. But she held her tongue and let Anna stay where she was. After all, wasn't Anna merely showing love in the most human way possible? Wasn't this the kind of love that we were trying to cultivate in our children all along?

After the bath, Liz sat Gaojie down at our kitchen table and served her a hot meal. While she ate, Liz told her all about Jesus, about who he was and how he loved her. Afterwards they prayed together, and as Lu Lu slept in her arms, Gaojie invited Jesus into her heart.

It is another of Liz's encounters, though, which I cherish the most, and which demonstrates how far a simple act of love can go.

One Friday towards the end of our first year in Beijing, in 2003, Liz had to run an errand early one morning. She was in a hurry and hadn't had time for breakfast, but there was a

McDonald's next to the bank where she had her meeting, so when she finished with the bank, she decided to pop in and grab something to eat. It was bitterly cold outside. Winter was coming and she was glad for the hot coffee to warm her up. As she sat at the table, sipping her coffee, she noticed a boy in his early teens cleaning the tables. She watched as he finished clearing up and it became apparent that he had done the work in exchange for a free burger and fries. She watched the manager hand him his burger, but rather than eat it, the boy put it into his pocket for later. In that moment, she felt a sudden wave of compassion for him.

She called him over so that she could speak to him.

His name, he said, was Zhou (pronounced 'Joe'). He claimed he was ten years old, but he was clearly a few years older than that.

Liz asked if he had somewhere to sleep. He shook his head. 'Would you like to come and stay with me and my family?' she said.

Zhou's eyes brightened and he nodded enthusiastically. Liz called me at once, and we agreed to let him stay while we figured out how we could help him.

In Beijing, we had a good-sized house again, with four bedrooms, in a development called Capital Paradise (or Ming Du Yen in Chinese). In addition, there were two rooms in the basement. Thomas Abbott, who was now working for Care for Children and had moved to Beijing with us, was in one. We gave Zhou the other.

The children accepted Zhou as a new addition to the family straight away, and they called him Joe. We made up a bed for him and found him some new clothes, but as the days went by he continued to be very guarded with us. He was hiding something, unwilling to share the whole truth about his life. I asked him how he came to be living on the streets in Beijing and he gave up little bits of his past, but never the whole story. Liz would tell Joe about Jesus, as she did with everyone she invited in the house, but he really didn't want to listen to that. He'd put his hands over his hears and shout, 'I hate Jesus!' He had quite a temper on him! Every now and then he would fly into a rage and smash things out of frustration.

Christmas was approaching, so we each decided to buy Joe a present that would be special for him. On Christmas morning, Joe woke late; he found it hard to sleep at night. On the streets he would stay up most of the night and sleep during the daytime; it was safer that way. Yet, even when he was safe under our roof, he would lie awake at night. One of the girls had had the idea of putting glow-in-the-dark stars on his ceiling, which he would stare at for hours. He loved them.

So, when he finally appeared on Christmas morning, hair at all angles and rubbing sleep from his eyes, we were all already downstairs in the sitting room. We sat him down, and one by one we all gave him our presents. He loved swimming, but he couldn't actually swim; he'd cling to me in the pool. So I gave him armbands. His face lit up when he tore off the wrapping and saw what they were. Josh and Joel gave him some Lego, knowing he loved to play with theirs. Liz and the girls each gave him a present that would mean something special to him. By the end of it all, Joe burst into tears. I don't think he had ever experienced even that token love.

'I don't think we've been loving him enough,' Liz said to me in a quiet moment, as we cleared away the reams of wrapping paper. I knew she was right. As soon as we went the extra mile, only then did he feel it was safe to let down his defences. Joe gave his life to Jesus that morning. And afterwards he told us his story.

He was, in fact, almost fourteen years old. (We all smiled when he said that, because it was pretty obvious he wasn't ten.) He admitted that, when he met Liz, he had told her he was younger because he didn't think she would want to help him if she knew his real age. He came from a village two hours south of Lanzhou city, in the province of Gansu. Gansu is sometimes called 'the neck' of China – long and thin, spanning the Silk Road heading west, away from civilisation, as the ancients saw it. It is one of the poorest provinces, and Lanzhou is one of the most polluted cities in the world.

Joe said his parents had divorced when he was a young boy. His brother went with his mother, and Joe went with his father. Pretty soon, his father remarried, and Joe's new stepmother had two sons of her own. The boys didn't get along at all, and their fighting caused a lot of angst and tension at home. When Joe was ten years old, his father took him to the local train station and abandoned him there. Having eventually realised what was going on, Joe managed to find his way back home. He banged on the door, begging to be let in. But his father just shouted at him to go away. 'We don't know you here!' he yelled.

Listening to this, my heart broke. It was almost impossible to imagine what that must do to a child, to hear words of such total rejection come out of a father's mouth. *We don't know you.* It made me shudder. At once, it made me think how the word of our Heavenly Father is the absolute inversion of that. *I know you. Welcome. Come in. We've been waiting for you. We have prepared a place for you.* As much as the word of rejection tears a heart in two, so the word of acceptance brings healing to that wound; I should know.

Acceptance *can* triumph over rejection, for all of us. Love can triumph over pain. We have seen it so many times.

Joe's story continued.

Rejected and alone, he didn't know what to do. In the end, he decided to go back to the station and get on the next train into the city. He snuck on a train to Lanzhou, and there he met a gang of street boys and joined them. They became his new family, and together they stole money to live. One day the gang decided to go to Shanghai, but when the other boys started to steal lead off roofs, Joe decided he needed to break away from them. He jumped on another train, this time to Beijing, once more avoiding the guards so that he didn't have to pay. There, he somehow scraped an existence, living on the streets. When Liz found him, he had been homeless in Beijing for three years.

He stayed with us for five months.

Gradually, over that time, he gave up more details about his family and where he had lived. One day, he let slip the name of the school he once went to. Our driver, Kong Ming, who you'll remember had also moved to Beijing with us, called the head-master of that school to see whether he remembered Joe. To our amazement, he did. He said that Joe was a very clever boy and he happened to know that his mother was still looking for him. He said, even those years later, she spent days at the train station, hoping Joe would turn up.

When we heard this, we decided that we needed to meet Joe's mother and see if Joe could go back to live with her. We knew he should be with his own family. It was Chinese New Year when we were finally able to arrange a visit to her in Gansu. But because that was the busiest time of year for travel, we simply couldn't find any tickets out of Beijing, whether by bus, train or plane. There were tickets still available, however, from his mother's home town to Beijing, so we bought one for her, and she came to stay with us for a week.

It was an extraordinary thing to witness the moment of their reunion. I went with Kong Ming to pick her up from the station so that the first time they could meet would be in the privacy of our home. Liz later told me that Joe was clearly excited at the prospect of her arrival, but also nervous, unable to sit still for a second until there was a knock at the door. She opened it, and there we were, with a small, neatly dressed woman of about thirty standing in the doorway. Joe's mother froze, her body seemingly caught between the emotion of seeing her son after so long and the formality of meeting the rest of us for the first time. I saw his face clearly. For a few seconds, he stood there, shaking like a leaf. Then she raised her arms to him and he ran to her and clung to her, his face buried in her shoulder and his back heaving with sobs.

I think we were probably all crying by then. It was an incredibly emotional experience, but so beautiful.

As the tidal wave of emotion subsided, we sat them down next to each other and they began to talk. Joe told her all that had happened to him, and ended by telling her about Jesus as well. It was amazing to hear him speak so tenderly about something so new to him. And I knew that, eventually, he would also bring his mother to the Lord.

Then his mother told us about her life, which sounded hardly less desperate than his. She had been selling her blood for money, and she was worried about Joe coming back to live with her. She was so poor that she could not afford to pay for electricity, so in the evenings, she said, he would not be able to do his homework. She knew he was clever and wanted him to succeed, and she feared that the life she could offer him would only hold him back.

It was a serious thing to consider, but on balance we still felt strongly that it was better for Joe to be with his mother, so we decided to pay for his school and her rent, which even for the whole year came to a very small sum. Even had it been a lot more, it would have been a privilege to help them. As it was, the cost to us of helping Joe and his mother was quite small, but the difference to them was huge.

It was a simple lesson to us. To anyone. But the truth of it was profound. It doesn't take a lot of love to turn around a person's life.

I could give you half a dozen more examples of Liz's generosity of spirit, of broken lives she helped set on the road to healing. Another involved a pitiful looking young man with one eye whom she came across. Liz was in a hurry, but she noticed him huddled on the side of the road. I had asked her not to bring male beggars back to the house unless she knew I was at home, because we need to have wisdom as well as compassion. So she told Kong Ming to tell the man to wait for me and that I would pick him up at 6.00 p.m. Jackie Pullinger had said that if someone is truly poor they will be willing to receive help. Kong Ming had to go past the street he was on a few more times that day, and he said the man never budged from his position.

At 6.00 p.m., on my way home, Kong Ming and I picked the man up and heard his story. He had been working on a building site for a year and earned 1,100RMB ($170) as his yearly wages. As it was winter and cold he decided to make his way south to Beijing, but on the outskirts someone pulled a knife on him and stole all his money. Left utterly penniless, he had been sleeping rough for three months in the freezing cold.

We picked him up and brought him some food, and I have never seen anyone eat so much so quickly. Next, we checked him into a warm local bed and breakfast, where he had a shower and changed into the new clothes we had bought him. His hair was still matted and long so we took him for a haircut, and I found him an old watch and an old wallet. He looked like a new man with his short back and sides, a nice suit, a Chairman Mao watch, and hand luggage with presents for all his family.

We knew enough about Chinese culture to know that he would not accept money as a gift. I had to get him to take the money but in a way that he could keep his honour. We told him the people who stole his money were wicked, but Jesus wanted to give it back to him. In winter, Chinese people wear two or three layers of clothes to keep warm. So we told him to put 100 yuan in his wallet and the rest in his inside trousers pocket so it wouldn't be stolen again.

That summer, we returned to the UK as a family to visit our parents. On our return to China there was a long letter on my desk addressed to 'Dear Aunty, Uncle and Jesus'. In it this young man told us that he had returned safely home and was so grateful that we had introduced him to Jesus, who he had now introduced to his mother, father, grandfather, grandmother, uncles and aunties . . . The letter went on to describe how half the village in which he lived had been introduced to Jesus!

Every story began in the same way. Liz had eyes to see the

'invisible' ones, the wretched poor who had fallen out of life. She had the feet to approach them, the hands to reach for them and the heart to love them.

I had much to learn from her.

18: Sichuan

Blessed are those who mourn,
for they will be comforted.
(Matthew 5:4)

In 2006, our contract with the CSWA was renewed for a further three years. This was the second big wave of expansion. The timescale for each project aimed for an initial partnership period of three years, after which we would step back and leave the running of each placement programme to the local orphanage authorities. Thus, as we came to the end of our involvement in the first wave of fifteen, we were freed up to begin engagement with the next fifteen projects that the Ministry of Civil Affairs had identified.

I won't list them. Suffice it to say they were mostly in the central, eastern and north-eastern provinces of China. One worth mentioning, though, was Harbin, often called the Ice City because of its famous annual ice-sculpting festival, which is located in the freezing far north-east.

The staff at the Harbin orphanage were worried that the children were too physically weak to be placed in families. The orphanages, at least, had central heating, but many of the homes they would go to did not. However, it happened that the orphanage director had once been a farmer, and he struck upon the ingenious notion of treating the children like the seeds of a crop.

'We will place the children in spring,' he told me. 'And like seeds, they will grow strong and hardy during the summer, so that they can bear the hard winter.'

Everyone agreed that this was a good idea, and in practice it worked perfectly. It's a nice example of the creative thinking that our work sometimes provoked in the different regions around the country.

In Beijing, during this time, it was hard to keep up with the pace of change. The Summer Olympics were getting closer, due to take place in August 2008, and the capital was not going to squander its opportunity to show the world how far China had come. Everywhere, extraordinary building projects were speeding ahead: stadiums, arenas, pool complexes, velodromes. And the rest of the city was being given an unprecedented makeover as well. Factories were moved outside the city limits to minimise the air pollution. The transport system was overhauled. I remember one mind-blowing occasion when we took the family to a nearby McDonald's on the subway. We came up out of the subway from one exit and went and had our meal. When we came back to get on the subway again, the exit we had used had vanished. Instead, a brand-new and perfectly functional exit had appeared, apparently out of nowhere, a block down the street, bright and shiny as a new toy.

Besides the building work, there were massive efforts to brighten up the city. Lamp posts were repainted. Gardens were replanted, parks were redesigned, thousands of ready-grown trees were brought into the city and planted. Everywhere was green. Everything was clean.

It was impressive. And all year in Beijing – in fact, all over China – you could sense the joy bubbling to the surface, the expectation that this was China's time to shine. At last it had come. Even for us as foreigners, the feeling of positivity was infectious; we wanted to see our Chinese friends have their moment of triumph.

And then . . . and then . . .

Mid-afternoon on 12 May 2008, news reports started flashing across the capital's TV screens and radio stations: 'Earthquake! An 8.0 magnitude on the Richter scale! Devastation in Sichuan! Tens of thousands missing!'

We had six partner orphanages in Sichuan, and at least a dozen placement projects. I called Sunny at once, who by this time was acting as our country manager.

'Have you got through to anyone?' I asked.

'No one,' he replied, his voice tense at the end of the phone. 'All the communication lines are down.'

The epicentre, he told me, had been about fifty miles to the north-west of Chengdu, in the rural countryside. The city itself had been shaken to pieces. Of course, at that early stage, the picture was very unclear, and the extent of the devastation was far beyond anyone's comprehension. As for the orphanages we had been partnering and their dozen placement projects spread across the province, we had no idea as to the fate of most of them – only that they would need our help.

'We're going,' I told him.

'I knew you'd say that. I've already reserved us tickets,' he said. 'We're flying tomorrow morning.'

'Good lad.'

We arrived in Chengdu airport very early on the second day. I'll never forget the scene that greeted us.

The concrete apron outside the terminal was packed with aeroplanes and air freight. Every half-minute or so another plane arrived, and the big airliners already on the ground had hardly shut down their engines before their cargo of aid matériel was hauled out of their holds and strewn on pallets across the tarmac. 'Matériel' is the right word: it felt like China had gone to war. Truck after truck drove into the mêlée to pick up the supplies – mostly food and water – and then sped out to the areas in desperate need.

In the terminal, the public TV screens were full of the scenes of the most harrowing destruction. There was no attempt to filter the footage that was coming out, nor the numbers of confirmed dead. There was a ticker in the top corner of every screen that just kept rising. (That went on for days.) The heart-rending agony of the disaster was laid out in all its gruesome reality. There was no sugar-coating this.

Sunny had managed to organise a government car to pick us up from the airport. As we drove into the city, we saw long convoys of ambulances that our driver said would have come all the way from Beijing or Shanghai. It was quite incredible to see the speed and extent to which China had mobilised its relief forces in Sichuan's hour of need.

A lot of the news coverage was focusing on the many schools that had been destroyed. One of the most horrific things about the earthquake was the time of day it had struck. At 2.30 p.m., most schools were still in session, while in the rural areas that were worst affected, the adults were out working in the fields. Because of this, there was a disproportionate number of children among the dead; school buildings had collapsed entirely, killing hundreds of children in a stroke. It was a heartbreaking theme to an already horrendous tragedy.

As more became known, the picture got worse. There were twenty-five suicides on the second day alone. People just couldn't handle the scale of their loss, with so many friends and loved ones just wiped away.

We drove straight to the Social Welfare Institute in Chengdu, our original orphanage partner in the province. There was some structural damage to the building – a large crack had opened up on the main façade – but it was still standing. The sight of that brought us some relief, but we found the staff in total shock. Each one of them was standing in front of the building in a circle, holding hands and singing, I think, a national song, only they were sort of wailing the song up into the sky, tears streaming down their faces. We slipped out of the car as discreetly as we could, but the orphanage director, who by now was a close friend, saw us. She ran up to me, shaking her head, unable to speak. I took her hand. She burst into tears, uncontrollable sobs racking through her. I must admit, it wasn't long before my own tears fell with hers. As the wave of her sorrow subsided, she was able to tell me that many of the staff had family members and friends who had died in the quake. Slowly, Sunny and I made our way round to each of the staff, hearing them tell story after story of loved ones who were dead or missing.

Sunny and I travelled on towards the epicentre of the earthquake to another orphanage in the town of Mingyang. As we drove further out of the city, the devastation in the landscape either side of the road grew worse and worse. It was stark and disturbing. Houses had been flattened into heaps of rubble. I remember seeing door frames still standing with the entire buildings around them vanished, as if by some conjurer's trick. Apartment blocks were cracked open like boiled eggs to reveal the wrecked interiors. Domestic scenes frozen in time – a kitchen table with plates still on it and chairs around it, but half the room torn away. Or beds hanging over the lip of a collapsed floor. An armchair on a balcony, filled with bricks. And the people we passed drifted like ghosts, many wandering around in a daze, perhaps still looking for their loved ones or else simply not knowing what to do with themselves, having lost everything and everyone. Others pawing weakly at a pile of rubble they used to call their home, or their child's school.

When we got to Mingyang, the orphanage building was still standing, although it was unstable, and the staff were starting to receive children from the worst hit areas surrounding them. The orphanages almost seemed to act as magnets for those in desperate need of relief supplies. There was so much trauma, it was hard to know where to start. Every person we met, whether adult or child, had their own story of having lost someone.

We heard that the hospitals were requesting assistance from trauma counsellors. I remembered Stephen Hyatt, a friend in Beijing and a clinical psychologist, who I knew was trained in trauma counselling. I called him and reported that there was a desperate need for him and others like him. He moved into action at once, mobilising other friends and associates with the necessary expertise, many of whom would spend numerous days in Chengdu and the surrounding region, counselling the bereft and training local medics and also some of our orphanage staff in the basics of how to handle such a huge outpouring of grief.

From Mingyang we drove on to Deyang, where another of our partner orphanages was located. Unlike the others, this orphanage building had been badly shaken by the earthquake. Most of the staff and children had been able to evacuate, but a few had been trapped inside the building on the second floor. Almost all the staff were female, but there was one man on site who acted as a sort of guard-cum-janitor-cum-gardener all in one. We heard how, when the building was still shaking, he ran back inside and up to the second floor where he found two babies who had been left behind. He scooped up one in each arm and, feeling more tremors hit the building, ran into the corridor only to see the stairs crumble away in front of him. Forced back into the dormitory, he saw that the only way out now was through the window, so he climbed onto the ledge and jumped down. Both children were saved, but he broke both his ankles in the fall.

The building was a wreck and too dangerous to re-enter. One of the supply trucks that pulled up every now and then had delivered tents to the orphanage, and these would be the orphans' new home for the foreseeable future. It was hardly ideal, but they were fortunate even to have that much. We were particularly worried about the children with additional needs because they were so much more at risk from the dangers around them. They had to be watched constantly.

It was May, which meant at least it was not too cold, but everywhere the children were dirty. With lots of flies and insects around, there was a serious danger of illness that could have easily grown into a localised epidemic. Sunny and I quickly realised that, aside from trauma counselling, what people needed in these more rural areas were the basics: shelter, food, water and a way to keep clean. On the drive back into Chengdu, we decided that the best way we could help was to mobilise 'health kits' through our Chinese and international partners back east.

One of Care for Children's partners was the Shangri-La hotel franchise. We were staying in its Chengdu hotel where already they had set up relief kitchens to supply the worst hit areas of the city and further afield. That first night, Chengdu was an eerily different city from the one I knew well. Everywhere people were camped outside on the streets and in the parks, afraid to go back into their buildings, even if they were still standing or apparently undamaged. Their fears had some justification: on the third day after the first tremors, the city experienced an aftershock which itself measured 6.4 on the Richter scale.

Stories started running on the media that the condition of Sichuan's buildings had been far below safety standards. Poorly maintained and with insufficient investment from the local authorities, they had been pitifully inadequate to withstand the might of such a massive earthquake. This shift in media opinion was extraordinary. China was wearing its heart on its sleeve, showing the world its pain. I actually believe, with hindsight, that this was a turning point in how media coverage in China has been done ever since. Emotions were running very high and there was criticism. But, at the same time, it seemed that nearly every part of Chinese society was willing to contribute to the aid effort. The Premier Hu Jintao addressed the nation every day for two weeks, briefing on the unfolding humanitarian crisis and what was being done to alleviate it. He struck upon a very practical solution: to designate individual cities around China to support specific towns in Sichuan that had been badly affected. This meant each city could give a very purposeful and focused response to each area in need.

Once we got on the phones to our various partners and supporters around China – the Carrefour supermarket in Chengdu itself, Virgin Atlantic and BP in Shanghai, as well as other Chinese companies and international schools in both Beijing and Shanghai – the response was immediate and effective. Word travelled fast. Carrefour started putting together plastic containers containing the basics – toothpaste, toothbrushes, socks, underpants, soap,

flannels – the health kits we had thought about. We then organised minibuses from the Chengdu orphanage to distribute them
all over the worst hit areas of the region. The Shangri-La gave us
a large conference room to use as a distribution centre.

Once the logistics began to come together, we were out every day,
delivering this aid, and often seeing the tragic carnage the earthquake
had left in its wake. Because of our connections with the provincial
orphanages we had special passes that enabled us to go through
the many roadblocks that the People's Liberation Army had erected
around Wenchuan, the epicentre of the quake. We were coming
and going from the worst hit areas every day, and I personally was
one of the few westerners permitted entry into the restricted zone.
This meant that every night when we returned to Chengdu, the
international press reporters, many of whom were staying in the
Shangri-La, were clamouring at me for an interview and eyewitness
report. One with whom I did several interviews was the American,
Anderson Cooper, who back then was reporting for ABC, but later
became well known as the news anchor for CNN.

They were long days. Hard days, physically and emotionally.
That first trip, we stayed, I think, for around a week. We managed
to visit all but one of our orphanage partners in Sichuan. The
last one was still undamaged, we heard, but the mountain pass
we needed to cross in order to reach it was blocked. It was some
months before Sunny was eventually able to visit them again. By
some miracle, none of the orphans in any of our partner orphanages was killed. But that didn't mean they weren't affected. As
I've said, almost all the staff had lost someone.

In one village where we were distributing our health kits, a
teenage boy approached me. He was in a complete daze, but we
started talking. He told me he had lost everyone: his grandparents,
his mother, his father, his brothers and sisters.

'Do you have any family left?' I asked, unable to get my mind
around the scale of tragedy this kid was facing.

He pointed vaguely to the horizon. 'You see those mountains?
I have an uncle who lives on the far side of them.'

It was a hot day. Both Sunny and I were sweating profusely from unloading the relief supplies. Suddenly the boy ran off, but he was back a minute later carrying bottled water for us. He handed it to us eagerly, encouraging us to drink. I couldn't believe it. After all this kid had been through – was still going through – he was still able to think of us and our thirst.

I asked Sunny how we could help him. Together, we got him to talk a bit more. He was a shy kid, with no real education. He said he wanted to be a long-distance haulage driver, so I asked Sunny to take his details, and we promised to help him. Care for Children would, in fact, go on to support him in obtaining his driving licence and the necessary qualifications to realise his ambition to be a lorry driver.

After that first trip, we made repeat trips of five or six days at a time for the next two months, continuing with the relief effort, liaising with the orphanages and overseeing the distribution of whatever aid we could get shipped in, thanks to our various sponsors. Among the things we ended up distributing were toys called MeiMei dolls. ('MeiMei' means 'little sister' in Chinese.) These were actually the product of a business idea Liz had come up with, having seen that the only dolls available in China seemed to be of western ethnicity in the style of Barbie – in other words, with long blond hair, white skin and blue eyes. Liz had found a manufacturer to make dolls that actually looked like ethnic Chinese, with black hair and the appropriate facial features. They were a poor substitute for the loss that many had experienced in Sichuan, but nevertheless they provided some small consolation to the girls in the orphanages and to the other traumatised children across Sichuan who were given one.

There is no doubt that the earthquake changed Sichuan for the worse. As well as the human loss and psychological scars left behind, something of the character of the land itself died. Sichuan used to be one of the most beautiful and picturesque provinces in China. The architecture in many of the villages was very traditional, a little antiquated, perhaps, but very distinctive and full of character. Much of that was flattened. Gone forever. In its place, they built concrete houses and high-rise apartment blocks, huge commercial centres and sprawling shopping malls. Sichuan was modernised in the blink of an eye, and not for the better. At least to my eye.

The shock waves of the disaster had spread throughout China. We were a grieving nation, a mood in no way helped by the barrage of graphic images that had been filling our news bulletins for weeks. As things began to stabilise in Sichuan and the focus returned to Beijing, there was still a sense that we had a lot of grief yet to process. I was invited on to China Central TV (CCTV) several times to participate in panel discussions about the concept of loss and bereavement and how people could begin to put their lives back together. There was a lot of healing to be done.

In some ways, the Beijing Olympics were a necessary and timely balm to the raw wound of Sichuan. A celebration of joy in answer to that terrible tragedy. And while the capital prepared to play host to the world, the Glovers had their own celebrations to attend to.

Thomas Abbott had first come into our lives in 2001. A visitor to the Hengshan Community Church, Thomas had been earmarked by Liz as a young man in need of some friends. He was in Shanghai to teach English, but as he grew closer to our family, he got to know us better. When he heard about the work I was doing, he asked whether he might have a job.

'Sure,' I told him. 'But I can only pay you a Chinese salary.'

That was fine by him. And before long, not only was he working for me, but he had also moved in with us as a lodger. Our eldest daughter, Rachel, was by that time doing her schooling in England. So for the first few years of their acquaintance, their friendship grew slowly of necessity, since they only saw each other when she was with us for the holidays. At a certain point, I forget exactly when, Thomas came to me and told me (very respectfully) that he wanted to explore being more than a friend to Rachel.

'Does she feel the same?' I asked.

He nodded.

'I suppose you'd better move out then,' I told him.

As I've said, Thomas moved up to Beijing with us, and it was obvious over the next few years that he and Rachel had found something that was going to last. So we were delighted when they announced they were getting married.

They had it all arranged. It was to be in London at Holy Trinity Brompton on Saturday 9 August 2008. When they told me the date, my heart sank.

'Hang on a minute,' I yelped. 'But the Opening Ceremony is on the eighth!'

The Olympics were scheduled to launch at 8.00 p.m. on the eighth day of the eighth month, 2008. The number eight is considered especially lucky in Chinese culture; there could be few more auspicious moments at which to declare the Games open.

'What about my tickets?' I wailed.

I had put my name in the lottery for event tickets, never dreaming that I'd be lucky enough to win two for the Opening Ceremony. That I *had* somehow won them, I could only explain as a miracle of God.

'Daaad,' said Rachel, glaring at me sternly, 'come on. Which is more important – your eldest daughter's wedding or tickets for some silly sporting event?'

Now, that was a tough question.

19: Beyond the Middle Kingdom: Thailand and North Korea

Do you see someone skilled in their work?
They will serve before kings;
they will not serve before officials of low rank.
(Proverbs 22:29)

By 2011, Care for Children was working with thirty-eight family placement project sites in twenty-seven different provinces, spanning the vastness of China. In thirteen years, we had grown from training in one orphanage in Shanghai to placing more than a quarter of a million children into families all across the nation. A multitude already, and a figure like that can impress, but when you think that each one is a child whose future has been changed, one of an abandoned generation who has been given back the chance to grow up in the love of a family, that's a lot of changed lives and a lot of different stories. And who knows? Perhaps it's enough to have set the story of China itself on a different course.

But it had become clear that God did not want Care for Children's work to remain behind the guarded walls of the so-called 'Middle Kingdom'. He had plans to break out.

India had been the wrong place at the wrong time. It's still my conviction that nothing about what we were doing in China would have worked in India. However, there was somewhere closer to home which, like a flower coming into bloom, had been opening up for some time, and where I was more confident that what we were doing could be replicated.

My connection with Thailand went right back to 2001, when I had attended a Tearfund HIV conference in Chiang Rai. It was there that I met Gary Haugen, who I believe later set up the International Justice Mission (IJM). Today, IJM works to combat the modern slavery and human trafficking that is driven by the sex industry. Back then, the issue was rife, and its insidious impact on Thailand made a deep impression on me. But it wasn't until a few years later that I felt the pull on our own activities to go there.

By then, we had been holding our biannual National Childcare Conference in Shanghai for three or four years. Although Thailand was outside China, we made a point of inviting state representatives from Thai orphanages to the event so that they could see what kind of changes to childcare were going on over the border. The Thai government was clearly interested, and from our side I had much greater confidence that what we were doing could work in Thailand (as opposed to in India), since the entire country was of a similar size to just one of China's many provinces. So the door was ajar. But it took another disaster for us to cross the threshold.

On Boxing Day 2004, we heard the news of the devastating tsunami that had hit the coasts of Thailand, Malaysia and Indonesia. As a family, we watched in horror at the footage of the mass of boiling seawater rushing inland. It was particularly poignant for us, since some of the footage included shots of the Holiday Inn in Phuket, where we had been on holiday as a family exactly a year earlier. We recognised the beach, the pool, the hotel. And all of it had now been destroyed.

During our holiday, we had met a French woman named Simone who worked for the Red Cross. We had kept in contact. When the tsunami hit, Simone set about organising aid for the victims. Part of the plan involved building a children's village for the newly orphaned children, and she invited Care for Children to come and see if we could help. I didn't want to do anything without the government's approval, since that had always been our modus operandi in China. So I contacted the Thai authorities and they arranged for me to meet Mr Wanlop, the Permanent

Secretary of the Ministry of Social Welfare, in Bangkok, before we travelled down to Phuket.

In March 2005, Liz and I found ourselves on a trip with the Red Cross, heading up the Thai coast to view the devastation. Besides the carnage I was later to witness in Sichuan, I have never seen anything like it. The scale of it was frightening, and strange. I remember seeing huge boats dumped on top of houses; a full-scale shipping tanker somehow was upended on the shoulder of a hill about two miles inland. I still struggle to comprehend the force of nature that must have carried it there.

As we drove through the affected areas, I realised that the region would be dealing with the aftermath of this for a generation to come.

When we finally caught up with Simone, she was still talking about the children's villages where she hoped to put all the orphaned children in one place to care for them all together. I suggested that this might not be the best way forward, and explained that it would be better to put our efforts into finding any surviving relatives and to place the children with them. We called that 'kinship care'. Once the children were safe with them, we could provide ongoing support through social workers. I told her that, in my professional opinion, this would be better for the children in the long run. She soon caught the idea, realising that once children found themselves in institutional care (in whatever form), it would be hard for them to get out of it again.

From that point, we started to explore the idea of extending our work beyond China. As with Shanghai, we would start by offering training to staff in the state-run orphanages of Bangkok.

However, it seemed the more we tried to engage, the more we became bogged down in bureaucratic detail. We were building relationships around the country, which was all to the good, and also within the Thai Ministry of Social Development and Human Security.

Three years later, we still seemed a long way off from implementing the first project in Thailand, wherever that would be.

So in 2008 we decided to inject the campaign with some new energy by holding a foster care conference in Bangkok aimed at the Southeast Asia region.

By this time, I had become acquainted with a man called Nick Chance, who held the office of Private Secretary to His Royal Highness Prince Michael of Kent. Nick had heard of our work in China and was keen to involve Prince Michael in any future efforts. (In time, the Prince would become the royal patron of Care for Children and Nick would eventually become one of our trustees.) The Prince had agreed to give a keynote address at the conference. He had actually already met with Yan Mingfu before this time, in China, and they had hit it off at once. Prince Michael is a fluent Russian speaker, and of course Yan Mingfu, having been Mao's Russian translator, is fluent in the language, too.

Having met Yan Mingfu, the Prince saw that Care for Children was operating at a very high level within the organs of government, so I think he took us far more seriously after that. In any case, Prince Michael said he was willing to help us, and realised that what he could do on our behalf was come to countries and apply whatever influence he had on their high-ranking persons of state, and hopefully open them up to our work. Thailand would be the tester for that.

As it turned out, it would set the bar pretty high.

So the Prince turned up and spoke at the conference in Bangkok. We then received word from one of the Thai officials that the King of Thailand wanted to give Prince Michael an audience. He asked me if I wanted to go with him. Of course, I was delighted. You have to realise that, at that time, the King of Thailand for the Thai people was effectively 'god', so here was a serious opportunity.

Initially, we were invited to go and lay a wreath for the King's sister, who had just died. After that, we were taken to the headquarters of the Army, where we were to inspect all the generals of the Thai Army, both of us sporting yellow ties (in honour of the Thai King, yellow being the colour of royalty there).

I realised as the inspection went on that time was running out. We needed to get back on the road if we were to keep our appointment with the King. When I mentioned this, one of the generals said, 'Oh, you don't need to worry about that. We can get you there in one of our helicopters.'

The day then took a turn for the surreal.

We were taken to a helipad, on which was waiting a Black Hawk helicopter, apparently the King's own aircraft, since inside was a throne on which the Prince was invited to sit. I sat with Nick Chance behind him. There were two special forces marines sitting on either side of the helicopter, armed with machine guns to protect us. We then flew for about half an hour, low over the jungle, and landed somewhere outside Hua Hin, where two gold Rolls Royces awaited our arrival. Nick insisted that I sat in the front car with the Prince, while he followed in the car behind.

We set out along the road, on which every fifty metres or so was another guard standing to attention and armed with a machine gun, and drove for about fifteen minutes to the royal palace. The palace sat on the seafront, overlooking a bay, the entrance to which was guarded by three warships. It was extraordinary – like a scene out of a Bond film, except even more over the top . . . beyond Bond, if you like.

We were greeted by one of the King's courtiers and taken for a walk around the palace grounds and then, eventually, brought into some kind of reception hall and invited to sit down. As we waited, in one of the most awkward moments of my life, we were served refreshments by some servants; but because we were seated and they couldn't be seen to be in any way superior to us, they had to crawl along the floor to serve us our drinks. It was truly bizarre. I felt very uncomfortable with that.

Now, an important detail of the story. Before we had gone to the palace, one of our trustees, Sir David Brewer, had told us that he, too, had once had an audience with the Thai King. He had a word of advice for us. 'If you want just five minutes, that's fine,' he said, 'that's all you'll get. But if you talk about dogs, you will be there the whole afternoon.'

David explained that the King of Thailand had sixty street dogs, which were like his babies. Armed with this piece of information, we waited for some time, and eventually the King made his entrance. There were formal introductions and then the King said to Prince Michael, 'Well, what have you been doing recently?'

'Oh, I've been up at Sandringham with my dogs,' replied the Prince, canny as ever.

'Do you like dogs?' The King's face lit up like a candle.

'I love dogs,' said the Prince warmly.

'Well, you'd better come along with me, then.' He led us into another grand hall where the centrepiece was a huge portrait of Red, his favourite dog. He then took the Prince off with him to the kennels to meet his dogs, leaving me with his personal assistant – a very charming man. We had a wonderful conversation during which I asked him, 'Have you worked for the King long?'

He said, 'I've given my life to the King. I've worked thirty-six years. I work an eighteen-hour day, and I've never had a day off. That is my privilege and service to the King.'

It was an amazing thought, but he didn't seem any the worse for it.

After some time the King and the Prince came back, and the King turned to me: 'Prince Michael has been telling me about the work of Care for Children. I would like you to start this work in Thailand.'

The next day we had a call from the Minister, Mr Wanlop, saying that they were now ready to sign the contract. The bureaucratic blockage had magically vanished overnight.

Things moved forward steadily after that. Steadily, but still rather slowly. There was a lot of preparation work to be done. We invited the key government officials to China in 2009, and then to our global conference in London in 2010.

The result of all our discussions and preparation was that it was agreed that the first project would be launched in the city of Chiang Mai in the north of Thailand. To mark the project launch, we held our biannual Childcare Conference in that city in late 2011, and the first Thai children were placed with families shortly after that.

The following year, Thomas and Rachel would move to Bangkok to open Care for Children's first permanent office there.

> *I will go before you*
> *and will level the mountains;*
> *I will break down gates of bronze*
> *and cut through bars of iron.*
> (Isaiah 45:2)

It was 2010 when I first heard of the North Koreans' interest in us.

To begin with, I wondered how they had even heard of Care for Children. But I soon realised that, since there were a number of North Korean diplomats and officials in Beijing, it would have been natural enough for them to want to know about child welfare in China, and any enquiry in that direction would have quickly brought up our name. It seemed the North Korean ambassador had requested that the Chinese introduce us to them. We were told that they wanted to explore the potential of establishing family care across their country.

As you probably know, North Korea is currently one of the most closed countries in the world, and has been for a long time. It is run on old-style Stalinist principles, and it is incredibly diffi-cult to obtain permission to work within its borders. Our first contact with the country was to host a delegation of North Korean officials in our offices in Beijing, where we held a series of meet-ings explaining what we had done and how we worked.

During the visit, as a bit of fun, we challenged the delegation to a table tennis match, since there was a table in our building. Four of our staff took on four of them. After three games, we were ahead, two games to one, and we still had our best player,

Emma Zhang, to come. She was a natural and was bound to wipe the floor with her opponent. I thought a timely word in her ear was necessary. 'You'd better give this one away, Emma,' I whispered. She duly complied, and the North Koreans were delighted to come away with an honourable draw. Face had been saved, which was probably just as well.

After the meetings were concluded, I received an official invitation to visit North Korea in December 2010. This time, my trusted companion, Sunny, was unable to come, since he was a Chinese national and, at that time, the North Koreans wouldn't grant him a visa. So in his place I took along Jason Tam, a physiotherapist from Hong Kong who was one of our training development managers. He was due to be married on the day we had been granted to enter the country. Since we didn't feel able to rock the bureaucratic boat by pushing back on our entry date, he got married in the morning and flew with me in the afternoon, which showed quite the commitment to the cause from him, I thought.

It was only a two-hour flight from Beijing to Pyongyang, but stepping off the plane was like stepping back in time. Naturally, we were escorted everywhere from the moment we left the aircraft. Driving into the city, we saw that there were hardly any cars on the roads, and those few we saw were antiquated. Everything was very quiet. The snow was already thick. The plainness of everything – the architecture, the roads, the clothes people were wearing – somehow reminded me of Scandinavia. It lacked that indefinable 'Asianness' that I was used to recognising everywhere in this part of the world. To give you some idea, each female staff member in the orphanages we visited wore a headscarf almost like a nun's wimple, with a frilly white pinafore. There were no mobile phones, no internet and only one TV station.

Most images we saw were of the dynasty that has been ruling North Korea since its founding in 1948. Kim Il-Sung, his son Kim Jong-Il, and now his grandson Kim Jong-Un. In 1998, Kim Il-Sung had posthumously been given the title Eternal President of the Republic, and his picture was everywhere, as well as all kinds of propaganda posters. There seemed to be a genuine fear that the Americans could invade at any moment. Someone told me that 60 per cent of the population was in the army, which staggered me. When asked, almost every child in the orphanage – boy or girl – said they wanted to be in the army when they were older. It was sad to see how confined their sense of the future was.

The trip was five days long. We hardly had a moment during that time out of sight of our government handlers. The first orphanage we visited in the capital was clean and well run. Better, in fact, than a lot of the places in China. Jason was able to demonstrate how to care for a baby girl with cerebral palsy. He showed the staff how to stretch her legs in such a way that she would engage the muscles that would then enable her to walk when she was older.

In one room, we were shown where the triplets were kept. There were three sets, all dressed in identical knitted jumpers and trousers. None of them was actually an orphan – their parents were alive and well. But President Kim Jong-Il had granted them special permission to put their children in residential care so that the state would bear the cost of raising them.

Besides the strangeness of the place, the people were extremely warm and friendly. All the same, there was no doubt I was an oddity there; people would gape at me in the streets. But they were open to a bit of fun. I got into a snowball fight with a rather precocious four-year-old at one point while we were waiting for our car to pick us up from the hotel. He was standing in a crowd of unsmiling Koreans, and when I saw him staring at me, I grinned at him and gave him a wave. With a mischievous look on his face, he snatched up some snow, and before I knew it he had run up and pelted me with a snowball, then fled in terror, squealing with delight. It wasn't long before we were in a full-on snowball fight, much to the amusement of the crowd. They seemed especially entertained when I let the kid smash a snowball in my face, clapping and laughing at the sight of a burly westerner being terrorised by their tiny countryman.

Later in the week, I happened to notice a football game going on across the street from our hotel. I had some spare time, so I wandered over to take a look. I found two girls' teams in the middle of a match. One team was losing very badly. With the bit of experience I have under my belt, I couldn't help noticing that the players on the team that was losing were all wrongly positioned. The smallest girl was in goal, they had a tough but slow girl up front, a tall girl on the wing who never got the ball and a slight girl in defence who kept getting steamrollered. At half time, they were 4–0 down.

I found a girl who could speak English and interrupted their half-time huddle, saying I had a couple of suggestions for them. At first they were a bit taken aback that a foreigner like me should take an interest in them and whether they won or not. But they listened to what I had to say and allowed me to reorganise them into more suitable positions, according to each one's size, shape and skill. The whistle for the second half had hardly blown than it was clear the team was markedly improved. They ended up winning the match 5–4. The girls were overjoyed, and I had a little spring in my step as I returned to my hotel.

On the last evening of our trip, we got back to the hotel, but I wasn't yet ready to turn in for the night. Even though it was a cold night, I fancied a walk. As I stepped outside, it began to snow. Flakes were falling in golden pools under the street lamps spaced along the road. It was so quiet, the snowfall so beautiful, that I pulled out my camera and started taking shots.

I ended up walking a few blocks, and when I reached the train station, a man in a leather jacket approached me. He was carrying a gun.

'What are you taking photos of?' he asked in English.

I was surprised to hear my own language, but his tone was good natured so I showed him my camera. He checked the few shots I'd taken and seemed satisfied that I was telling the truth.

'I think it's time you went back to your hotel,' he said. 'Don't you?'

I realised I ought to do as he said.

When I reached the hotel lobby, Jason and our minders had been about to get in a car to come and find me.

'What did you do?' he exclaimed, looking a bit fraught.

'Nothing much,' I shrugged. 'Just stretching the legs.'

It seemed that in the short time it had taken me to walk back to the hotel, the man I had met had already somehow found out everything about me and had mobilised my minders to find me and get me off the street. I suppose I should have been grateful. People have been locked up in North Korea for less.

As a pathfinder mission, that first trip to Pyongyang was a success. We visited a number of orphanages, visited various important people and did a lot of talking and selling the idea of family placement. It enabled us to form some relationships with our North Korean contacts, and it also gave us a sense of what we were dealing with there.

Our second trip involved more detailed discussions about training, vetting processes and how we might set up a programme in partnership with the state authorities that would work for them. On this visit they told us they were keen to send a small team of athletes to the London Paralympics in 2012. We offered to help them secure funding to make that happen. It would be the first time the DPRK had been represented in the Paralympics.

In the end, their team of three athletes shrank to just one swimmer, a man who had lost an arm and a leg in a terrible accident. We organised a fundraising dinner in London, hosting a delegation from the DPRK and a gathering of Care for Children's friends and supporters. This went down very well with our North Korean partners.

A few days before the lone swimmer was due to compete, I discovered he had only very recently learned how to swim. I watched him compete with my heart in my mouth, fearful that some disaster might unfold before the eyes of the world. I breathed a huge sigh of relief when he reached the finish line. I'm pleased to say he didn't drown, although he did finish last by some considerable distance, albeit to a standing ovation. In fact, his efforts became rather iconic of the whole ethos of the Games.

On our final trip to Pyongyang, we were still there when the stand-off between North and South Korea blew up into a full-on confrontation. North Korea had launched some missiles. South Korea had put its forces on high alert. There was a real danger that the crisis could escalate into all-out war. I realised then that just by being there, we were putting our people at unnecessary risk, so we changed our approach. Instead of us going in, we encouraged the North Korean orphanage staff to come out. We invited them to the regional training workshops we would hold periodically in north-east China.

To this day, we continue to support them in that way in their efforts to find families to love and care for those orphans hidden away in that shadowy corner of the world. It's my prayer that they will see the same change come about in their nation that we have seen all across China.

Epilogue: Counting Stars

Now to him who is able to do immeasurably more
than all we ask or imagine, according to his
power that is at work within us, to him be glory . . .
(Ephesians 3:20–21)

Liz and I left China in 2013.

By then, all our daughters had flown away west, except Rachel and Thomas in Thailand. When our twin boys, Josh and Joel, left Beijing to go to university in England, Liz and I felt it was the right time to return home. There's something about having your family around you. It gives you a unity of purpose. Without them, it's easy to lose your sense of direction.

There were other reasons to go back to the West. Up until that point, all of Care for Children's finances had been audited in China. We had a small UK office based in Norwich by then, but they were finding it more and more difficult to make sense of finances that were audited according to a totally different accounting system. We needed to gravitate our finances back to the UK to alleviate this problem. Also, with Thailand opening up and other countries on the horizon, we wanted to tighten the focus on the UK as the main base of operations for Care for Children, rather than continuing to be centred out of China. Aside from that, we wanted to be back home to support our family – not only our children, but also our parents who were becoming increasingly elderly.

So we returned to the land of our past with our eyes on the future.

In the years that followed, Care for Children's reach would expand further still, into Vietnam and Cambodia. And there have been many flights back and forth from China, from Hong Kong, from Bangkok. From all over Asia.

In October 2015, the Chinese news agency Xinhua announced the plans of the government to abolish the one-child policy. All families would now be allowed to have two children. It cited a communiqué issued by the Communist Party: 'to improve the balanced development of population' – an apparent reference to the country's female-to-male ratio – and to deal with the ageing population The new law took effect on 1 January 2016 after it was passed in the standing committee of the National People's Congress on 27 December 2015.

When I had first arrived in China, twenty-odd years earlier, there had been a generation of orphans destined for institutional care, thanks to that same policy. An abandoned generation. By redirecting that destiny into family care, we changed the nation.

There is a quote I used to share with my Chinese colleagues, which I attributed to Churchill because I knew he was a leader they deeply respect: 'The greatness of a nation can be judged by how it treats its weakest members. The mark of a great leader is the same.'*

Here were the weakest and the least in Chinese society: orphans who had been discarded and cast aside simply for having come into existence. Now, children who had been rejected or who had lost their biological parents had been given hope by men with the heart of a father and women with a mother's heart to draw close and love children who were not their own. I believe that drawing these 'weakest ones' back into the richness of Chinese family life will change the heart of that nation for ever.

Today we are working towards creating a digital legacy in China, a legacy of online knowhow that multiplies everything that we have learned and everything we have sought to impart. All the

---

* It was Mahatma Ghandi who said, 'A nation's greatness is measured by how it treats its weakest members.' I believe Churchill changed 'nation' to 'leader'.

legislation is now passed; all the regulations are in place. The change has come. And I pray it will endure.

In October 2018, we held the Pan-Asia Family Placement Conference in Shanghai, where it had all begun almost exactly twenty years before. I had invited Su Yiya to address the delegates. He was one of the original children from the very first batch of orphans we had placed. Now a young man of twenty-nine, and already carving out a successful career as a partner in the huge investment conglomerate Tencent, for whom he runs WeChat, China's answer to Facebook, Twitter and Instagram rolled into one, Su Yiya spoke with a style and confidence that left many in tears as they heard of a life transformed by years of dedicated love. It was an incredible testimony to the positive outcomes of a loving family life.

As the applause died down, another man, Professor Qu of the Beijing Bureau of Statistics, stepped up to the podium to speak. 'Today in China, 85 per cent of the children in care are living in families,' he said.

In 1996, there was not even a word for family-based care; now, the majority of orphans growing up in China would do so in the bosom of a loving family.

I stood up. I had one question that was burning on my heart. 'Professor Qu,' I said, 'forgive the interruption. Are you able to give us the total figure?'

'I'm sorry, I don't understand. This *is* the total of all those children currently in care.'

'Currently, yes,' I replied. 'But how many since the beginning? Since those first children, like our friend here.' I gestured at Su Yiya.

The professor adjusted his glasses. 'It would be hard to say. I don't have the figures–'

'Roughly, then,' I pressed him. 'An educated guess.'

'Mmm,' hummed the professor. 'If pushed, I would guess . . . more than one million children.'

Afterwards I sought out Yan Mingfu among the crowd of

delegates. When I found him, we looked at each other, smiling. Then he held out his hand and I shook it once more.

Nothing else needed to be said.

Yang Jia is a little village set high on a mountain plateau, floating in the clouds above the green hills of Yunnan.

Liz and I have returned here as part of a documentary film project called *Children of Shanghai,* which we are making with the BBC producer, Richard Nash. David Devenish is with us, the man whose word of prophecy began so much for me and my family: *You are going to be a father to as many children as there are stars in the sky.*

David has planted hundreds of churches throughout Europe and Asia. His wisdom, encouragement and friendship over the years have been very precious to me. Also with us is Francis Chan, a man whose passion for the Church, for God and for making disciples has had a great impact on me.

The people of Yang Jia are from the Yi and Lisu tribes. Most families in the village are farmers. The community is poor. It's September. Our bones are still rattling from the three-hour drive from the city of Kunming up to the plateau. But the day is warm for now, and the sun still bright.

An old man sits on a long, wooden bench outside his house, watching drowsily as we spill out of the orphanage truck. I recognise him, smile and go over to him. We start talking. I ask him to tell me his story again, and throw a nod at the camera behind me. He doesn't seem to mind. He says that his grandfather became a Christian a long time ago, when a young Englishman came to live in their village.

'My grandfather was the only one to listen to him. He became a follower of Jesus. He had a difficult time for many years. People mocked him. Sometimes worse.' We listen as the old man explains how his own father then started a small church in the village, and how finally he himself took over its running. 'During my lifetime,' he says, 'the whole village has become Christian.'

As a community, they decided to invite all the disabled children from the Kunming orphanage into their homes. In all, seventy families, all of them Christian, have given homes to more than 160 children with additional needs.

On the plateau, when the sun falls, the nights are cold. That evening our hosts put on a performance for us. There is dance and song, they make music and recite ancient poems. The children are given prime billing, as much a part of the community as anyone else. The adults encourage the children, clapping and laughing with them, speaking words of affirmation.

'I love my family!' declares one little boy. He has Down's syndrome and is grinning from ear to ear. 'I love my Mum and Dad!'

'Every child, every person needs to know that they are a source of joy,' I once read. 'Every child, every person needs to be celebrated. Only when all of our weaknesses are accepted as part of our humanity can our negative, broken self-images be transformed.' The village of Yang Jia demonstrates the truth of those words.

Jesus said, 'By this everyone will know that you are my disciples, if you love one another' (John 13:35).

Here, mothers, fathers, grandparents, aunts and uncles, brothers and sisters all work together to include the orphans and abandoned children in their lives.

'I've been to a lot of places around the world,' Francis Chan says to me, as we look from face to face around the gathering. 'But I don't think I've ever seen a more beautiful group of people.'

This was the dream that God put in my heart. This was why he brought me to China.

The work isn't over. Our goal, our passion, is to help hundreds of thousands more children across Asia find their place in a family. To change the lives of children, and so the future of nations.

As for my family, we have had the privilege of witnessing the meteoric rise of one of the great nations of the earth. We have seen spiritual revival in the Christian Church on a scale never before imagined. And we ourselves have been on a remarkable journey of faith. Each one of us. God has given us the grace to be part of his adventure and his plan.

None of this would have been possible without my wife, Elizabeth – without her faith, without her courage, without her compassion for the poor. The legacy of her expansive heart is there for all to see in the lives of our children. I know her sacrifice has been great, and the challenges she has faced have been enormous.

We often say that, in those early years, it was as if God had placed our family within a spiritual bubble, the Holy Spirit protecting and guiding us as we felt our way forward. God has blessed us far beyond what we ever thought possible. And as I look at the lives of my children, all of them now adults and embarking on their own adventures, I smile and I thank God for each of them.

I also ask myself sometimes whether we did the right thing for *them*. The answer to that question lies in the heart that God has given each one of them, and in the grace that is on their lives. And so I am satisfied and grateful. As a father, I've often struggled with their boldness of faith and find myself trying to bridle the risks that they are willing to take. Then I hear them say, 'But you didn't do it that way, Dad, did you?'

And they've got me.

I didn't. So why should they?

Why should you?

Now to him who is able to do immeasurably more than all we ask or imagine, according to his power that is at work within us, to him be glory in the church and in Christ Jesus throughout all generations, for ever and ever! Amen.

(Ephesians 3:20–21)

HODDER &
STOUGHTON

Hodder & Stoughton is the UK's
leading Christian publisher,
with a wide range of books from
the bestselling authors in the UK
and around the world ranging from
Christian lifestyle and theology to
apologetics, testimony and fiction.
We also publish the world's
most popular Bible translation
in modern English, the New
International Version, renowned
for its accuracy and readability.

Hodderfaith.com   Hodderbibles.co.uk
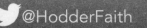 @HodderFaith    /HodderFaith